MW01127182

A VIEW FROM THE HILLS

THOMAS GARRETT

Merry Christmas!
I hope you enjoy these
little looks at life.

Thomas "Sonny" Garrett

Outskirts Press, Inc.
Denver, Colorado

The opinions expressed in this manuscript are solely the opinions of the author
and do not represent the opinions or thoughts of the publisher.

A View from the Hills
All Rights Reserved
Copyright © 2007 Thomas Garrett
V 2.0

This book may not be reproduced, transmitted, or stored in whole or in part by
any means, including graphic, electronic, or mechanical without the express
written consent of the publisher except in the case of brief quotations embod-
ied in critical articles and reviews.

Outskirts Press
http://www.outskirtspress.com

ISBN-10: 1-4327-0516-4
ISBN-13: 978-1-4327-0516-9

Outskirts Press and the "OP" logo are trademarks belonging to
Outskirts Press, Inc.

Printed in the United States of America

PROLOGUE

The articles including "Odds & Ends" are reprinted herein with the permission of *The Baxter Bulletin* for whom they were originally written. The articles have been published for *The Baxter Bulletin* continuously since 1983.

ACKNOWLEDGEMENTS

I started writing "Odds & Ends" at *The Baxter Bulletin* in 1983, five years after I started working at the paper. It seemed like a good idea at the time, and I've been writing the column for 24 years. When I began, I wanted to offer my two cents' worth about what was going on around Mountain Home, the Ozarks and Arkansas. As time progressed, I branched out to touch on subjects near and far, from offering occasional political commentary to sharing memories and observations on family, growing up in Texas, finding a good hamburger and just the odds and ends of life in general.

What follows is a sampling from among those columns. This collection features some of the ones from the early years and some more recent columns. Some are humorous (I hope), some are nostalgic (with the intervening years making them even more so) and a few are serious. Some show their age, but also remind us of changes that have taken place since I started writing "Odds & Ends." Occasionally, I've added notes to put columns into context and to help explain what I was thinking at the time (although I must admit after rereading a few even I wonder what

I was thinking at the time).

I owe so much to so many people for making this collection possible, for their encouragement, support and inspiration. It's hard to dedicate this to any one person, so just let me mention a few I count as instrumental.

- Dora Rumsey and Doris McCrary, two of my English teachers at DeKalb High School who opened new horizons to me in reading and writing.
- Janet Nelson, the former *Baxter Bulletin* editor who hired me at the newspaper and gave me a chance to become a columnist.
- Richard A. Knaak, an author and friend who, whether he knows it or not, lit the spark several years ago that led to this book.
- The Baxter County Library, for keeping better track of my columns than I did thanks to microfilm.
- Dad and Mom, Tommy and Frances Garrett, for all they gave me in life, the lessons they taught, the inspiration they provided. If not for them, none of this would have been possible, and I know they're still with me.
- And, of course, Kim, Amelia and Eli, for putting up with me all these years. I'm not the easiest person in the world to live with, but they've stuck by me. Thanks.

I hope you enjoy these ramblings, that they bring you a smile, a memory, maybe even a tear, Thank you for giving me some of your time.

CHAPTER 1
LIFE AS I SEE IT
LAND YACHTS

Like sunburn and chiggers, the return of tourists marks the beginning of another summer. Already thousands of these annual visitors have descended on our fair community. If the Memorial Day Weekend two weeks ago was any indication, we should have a bumper crop.

Some of these tourists claim to be campers, yet they journey to various parts of the country in their 80-foot land yachts.

Land yachts, for those unfamiliar with the name, are those self-contained homes-on-wheels you see people herding down the highways. They look like a cross between a shotgun house and a Greyhound bus. These wonders of modern Detroit know-how contain everything right down to the kitchen sink and can sleep the entire Osmond and King families.

Every summer, families across the nation roll their land yachts out of dry-dock and buy out the nearest filling station to get it fueled up. With bicycles strapped across the land yacht's front grill, minibikes lashed onto the rear bumper and a small foreign car in tow, our intrepid travelers set forth in search of the great outdoors.

Usually, they make it to the end of the block before having to gas up again.

Refueled, the land yacht zooms along the highway at 35 miles an hour, 40 if there's a strong tail wind. However, when it starts up hills of any size, generally any elevation one degree above level, the speed drops drastically. This always endears the pilot of the land yacht to all the line of drivers behind him.

Of course, during these interludes the drivers following the land yacht get a chance to read the little signs usually found on the back of such vehicles, signs which say such things as "Fred & Wilma, South Northeastern, Ill. Spending Our Children's Inheritance."

Clearing the hills, the captain sets course for the nearest campground. Not just any campground, mind you, but one whose spaces have electrical hook-ups, water connections, cable connections, concrete foundations and validated parking.

After getting it squeezed between the tree-to-tree land yachts already anchored there and making all the connections, it's time to enjoy nature.

Our erstwhile adventurer settles into his genuine imitation plastic chaise lounge with a cooler filled with an assortment of libations, sets a portable color television on his lap, tunes in the nearest station carrying the Cubs and enjoys life.

The kids busy themselves chasing chipmunks and skunks around their fellow land yachters' vessels and riding minibikes across picnic tables. Meanwhile, the wife, too, is enjoying this communion with nature.

Always glad for the opportunity to escape household chores, she spends her time cooking meals, washing dishes, cleaning the land yacht, picking up after her husband and children and generally having a carefree vacation.

Night comes, and they all climb into their land yacht, turn on the air conditioner, switch on the TV and shut out the sound of those pesky crickets and frogs.

Alas, the day comes when it's time to weigh anchor and set sail for home. But our land yachters will have memories of this trip to last a lifetime.

And gasoline bills and monthly payments on their vessel, which will last almost as long.

CHAPTER 2
THE OFFER OF A LIFETIME

The phone rings. It's after 9:30 at night, so it probably isn't good news.

I'm right.

"Hello, Mr. Garrett? I'm Ann Oying with Lifetime Publications, We're offering a brand new series of books about the lifestyles of insects called 'The Crawly World,' and we wondered if you'd be interested in it?

"Well …"

"Excellent! Now, we'll send you the first volume in this exciting series, 'Mosquitoes – Mother Nature's Dive Bombers,' for a 10-hour free examination. If you like the book, just send $14.95, plus $2.13 to cover postage and handling along with $50 to cover our phone bill, and we'll start sending you the others in this fascinating serried."

"Look, …"

"Fantastic, Mr. Garrett! Just listen to what Lifetime Publications offers you. Every two days, we'll send you another edition in our insect series at the same low price as our introductory book.

Future entries in the series will include 'Ant Against Ant – The Story of Insect Warfare During the 1860s,' 'Killer Bees – Hit or Myth?' 'Praying Mantis – Religion Among Insects.' Don't these sound exciting?"

"Not really."

"Great! Now, I want to remind you that Lifetime Publications also offers a variety of other services. Among some of our more popular series are 'The Old East,' 'The History of Popsicle Architecture,' 'The Life of Millard Fillmore' and our ever popular 'Home Repairs for Incompetents.' Yes, after reading the books in that last series even someone who doesn't know the difference between a hammer and a left-handed monkey wrench will be able to build their very own Taj Mahal right in their own backyard."

"Look, about your offer, I'm really not …

"Wonderful! I knew you'd like this exciting offer. Why, everyone I've called tonight has accepted it. They just can't get enough of our books. In fact, we're thinking about bringing out 412 new series just for your part of the country alone. Doesn't that just send chills up your spine?"

"It certainly does."

"Super! Say, do you think you might be interested in some of the ones we're planning? "I don't think so."

"Beautiful! I'll just make a note beside your phone number, Mr. Garrett, so we'll remember to call when those books start coming out next week.

By the way, have you seen our commercials on television?

"You mean the ones that tell me everything I don't want to know about your books?

"That's right! Oh, Mr. Garrett, if you've seen those then you're eligible for our special free gift, a 99-year trial subscription to our special magazine, 'Useless Information Weekly.' There is, however, a $3,217.99 handling charge."

"I'm thrilled."

"Wonderful! Now, let me make sure we have your correct address. Thomas Garrett, Mountain Home, Arizona."

"Arizona?"

"Arizona, that's what the Postal Service abbreviation shows as your address."

"Why yes, ma'am, that's correct. Just send it to Arizona."

CHAPTER 3
BETWEEN THE LINES

(Obviously, this one is a few years old. For those who don't remember, or are too young to know, it's Walter Mondale and Gary Hart, two casualties of presidential politics. The ideas still remain viable, however.)

As anyone who hasn't been wintering in Bimini or living in a cave on the Buffalo River has noticed, the election year is in full swing. There probably are as many candidates running around the country as Carter has little liver pills.

Each election brings its own share of humor, although those with their feet in their mouths usually don't think it's very funny. Some of the humor is unintentional, like watching candidates backtrack, trying to talk their way out of something they shouldn't have been in in the first place.

Some is intentional.

My personal favorite intentional political humor took place during the last election in a Colo-

rado community where people upset with the un-
challenged district attorney ran their own con-
tender – Sal A. Mander. The incumbent didn't see
the humor, and on election night blocked the release of the results, which indicated one mythical
Mr. Mander may have indeed outpolled the actual,
living incumbent.

After about the first two months of political
campaigns, anyone who's followed the activity can
give candidates' speeches for them since they already know what the would-be officeholders are
going to say, especially those running on the national level. After all, they've made the comments
so many times before even a mynah bird could
quote the speeches word-for-word.

The real trick, however, is not in memorizing
the speeches. No, the real trick is translating what
the politicians are saying into real language.

For example, Mondale says he thinks he's still
the frontrunner, and that he will beat Hart. What
Mondale really is saying is he's scared witless and
may have to hire someone to break Hart's legs, or
else all his work will go down the porcelain convenience.

There are other standard phrases tossed out by
politicians that have other meanings. For example:

- "I don't think you can really rely on polls
  for an accurate reading of the people's feelings." Translation: "I might not be able to
  change a light bulb without an electrician,
  but I'm still smarter than my opponent."

- "This is only a minor setback. We still have several more primaries, and I think we'll do better in those." Translation: "I'm so far behind all I can see is heels and elbows."
- "My opponent is an honorable man, and I wouldn't do anything to besmirch his reputation." Translation: This guy's lower than a snake's belly and slimier than a snail's trail, and as soon as my campaign staff digs up enough dirt, I'll leak it to the National Enquirer."
- "Well, we may not have as much money as our opponent, but I think that'll change as we gather momentum." Translation: "I've hocked everything except my wife and kids, and they're on the line now that I've borrowed funds from Godfather Savings and Loan of Chicago."
- "It's time for a change, and I think I'm more qualified to give the people what they want." Translation: "I might not be able to change a light bulb without an electrician, but I'm still smarter than my opponent.
- "I see economics as the main issue of this campaign. Translation: "If I don't win this election, I'll be standing in the unemployment line."
- "Well, I gave it my best shot." Translation: "If the people aren't smart enough to vote for me, then they deserve what they get."

- "I urge my supporters to get behind my opponent." Translation: "And push him off the nearest cliff."

And so it goes.

CHAPTER 4
TO CAP IT ALL OFF

(Little did I know what the future would hold when I wrote this.)

While wandering past one of the stores on the square the other day, I noticed a sign in the window announcing a contest sponsored by Levis to pick the 1984 U.S. Olympic Team uniform. I pondered this all-important question for a while – about 30 seconds – and couldn't think of any unique American clothing which would allow our athletes to stand out from the crowd.

Then it suddenly dawned on me that there is indeed something, a uniquely American form of headwear that could be suitable for the Olympians.

The gimme cap.

"Wait a minute. Just what in the wide, wide world of sports is a gimme cap?" you're wondering.

The gimme cap, according to social and fashion historians, originated in the farm and ranch industry. A few years ago, a manufacturer of feed, seed and fertilizer came up with the idea of putting his product's name on caps. These caps were for farmers and ranchers who bought its product. The farmer had something to protect him from the sun, and the company had its product promoted every time the farmer wore his cap.

The name originated when a farmer, having just purchased a season's supply of fertilizer, noticed the caps on a shelf behind the counter and uttered the immortal phrase:

"Gimme one of them caps."

Thus, the gimme cap was born, and American advertising had another success story. Nowadays, farmers, truckers, carpenters, fishermen, layabouts and almost anyone you meet on the square wear gimme caps.

I've collected a few gimme caps bearing the names of various country music stars I've seen in concert and places I've visited. One of my cousins has a fair-sized collection of gimme caps obtained from different companies in the oil industry, farming and other enterprises. His wife, however, has threatened him with bodily injury if he brings home one more gimme cap.

Over the years, the gimme cap has gone in many directions. You still can get ones with names of feed, seed and fertilizer, but you also can get gimme caps with the names of automobiles, trucks, motorcycles, boats, planes, towns, recreation parks, resorts, stores, snuff and musicians emblazoned upon them. A few have slogans or expressions written on them, some of which shouldn't be seen in mixed company.

Unfortunately, as more and more people became involved in producing gimme caps, an insidious change took place. Now, unless you've made some enormous purchase, when you say, "Gimme one of those caps," the man behind the counter says, "Gimme five bucks."

But, back to the Olympians. I think the gimme cap would complement their uniforms perfectly. They could wear an assortment of gimme caps with several different logos and names on them to the various events. It would be a perfect example of the American free enterprise system at work and would give many companies a shot at opening worldwide markets for their products.

Besides, can you imagine the envy they would generate within a foreign athlete who would long to live in America so he, too, could have his own Whitfield Farm Supply cap?

CHAPTER 5
INTRODUCING
THE MACHOMOBILE

I was thumbing through a car magazine the other night and came across an article about car names. It told how some models got their names, mentioned the names of vehicles that haven't existed in decades and listed a few names that had been considered for automobiles.

It was pretty interesting to learn that the Camaro got its name almost at the last minute before production began and almost by accident. It seems somebody with Chevrolet was looking through the "C"s in a dictionary when he came across the word. Thus, one of the top-selling sport models got its name. Unfortunately, I've forgotten what it originally meant, but now it means "fast Chevy."

I found that Ford can't call its Mustang by that name in Germany because it's already registered there as the name of a lawn mower. That probably would cause shock among any American who ordered a Mustang in Berlin and instead of getting a sleek car wound up with a Deutsch equivalent of a Snapper.

Despite my brief synopsis of that article, it was an interesting piece of writing. And, naturally, I began thinking about names for vehicles. In our society, cars, like pets, seem to take on characteristics of their owners, which probably doesn't say a whole lot for me considering the current state of my Green Bomb.

Anyway, I started trying to come up with a few vehicle names that would match their owners.

For example, Machomobile. Now, a Machomobile would have enough horsepower to move a battleship, glow-in-the-dark racing stripes, two-foot wide slick rear tires, a jacked-up rear end six feet above the ground and no mufflers. It would be driven by young men trying to impress young ladies by driving back and forth through the gas pumps at the Gulf station.

If that's not your speed, try the Punkster. This is a car built to look like a '52 Dodge and would be two-tone – rust red and primer gray. It would have at least one side bashed in, a crack in the front window, a piece of cardboard for the driver's window and its exhaust would spew forth enough fumes to choke Los Angeles. Despite these apparent flaws, the vehicle would have a car stereo whose volume control adjusts to Loud, Louder and Crumble Buildings. The latter setting is only used when the driver is stopped at a traffic signal.

In the trunk would be a complete set of burglar tools and somebody else's spare tire. The

Punkster would be driven by someone who looks like he shouldn't be eligible for parole yet.

Then there's the Good Ol' Boy 4WD. This would be a four-wheel drive truck whose standard equipment would include an easy rider rifle rack in the rear window, a Skoal bumper sticker, fog lights – both front and rear – chrome running boards, reflector mud flaps and a 12-foot whip antenna. It would be driven by folks in cowboy hats and whose favorite hobby is stomping the drivers of Punksters

Next is the Pasadena. This vehicle would go no faster than 15 mph, have orthopedic seat covers and could only be driven down the middle of the center line on any roadway. Its driver would barely be able to peek over the steering wheel and usually would get caught at the stoplight surrounded by the Machomobile, Punkster and Good Ol' Boy.

I have my doubts that Detroit would be interested in these names or vehicles, although anyone who gets on the road might think they're already in production.

(And then came the Hummer and the SUV.)

CHAPTER 6
CAUTION: LIFE MAY BE UNHEALTHY

I t seems every day there's a new pronouncement about things that are bad for us, and things researchers aren't sure about, but they certainly must not be good for us.

When I looked at the AP wire this morning, there wasn't just the daily story about an announcement of a new finding that something else is bad for us. There was a 14-inch list of pronouncements made in just one day. It was Christmas in November for folks who love hearing such news.

Here's just a sample of the latest things we need to be aware of found in that one wire story.

- A nutrition group, saying there was "a public health scandal in the making," requested an improved federal inspection program for seafood because Americans are at increased risk from bacterial, viral and toxic contamination. Now, that's great news, coming as it did the day after another report said fish oil and eating more seafood are good for people.

- Smokers who cut back on doctors' orders may compensate by smoking more intensely, tripling the tar and nicotine they inhale. In other words, they inhale with enough suction to take the chrome off a trailer hitch.

- Teenage boys with elevated levels of sex hormones may be at increased risk for heart disease later in life, but the findings may be useful in predicting which ones will have heart disease, allowing preventive measures. On top of puberty, 14-year-old boys now have to worry about heart disease, too.

- Men who are not physically fit are more than four times as likely to die of a heart attack as men who are fit. Does this mean, healthwise, one Arnold Schwarzenegger equals four Woody Allens?

- People who snore have narrower throats than those who sleep quietly, and doctors say this may be one of the causes of their nightly rumbles and snorts. Of course, it's also easier for the spouse of a snorer to get his/her hands around narrower throats.

Isn't all that nice news to wake up to in the morning? With all those other pronouncements we hear every day, you have to wonder what to make of these developments.

I suppose the pessimist could look at this and say when men who had high hormone levels as teenagers who smoke any amount of anything, who eat uninspected cod, who get no exercise and sound like a low-flying formation of B-52s at night probably have about 30 seconds to live.

The optimist, however, sees this as proof that clean living, fresh air, exercise, eating properly, inspected flounder and not snoring should add more years than Methuselah had to his life.

Personally, I'm not sure what to make of all this. I have no doubt that improving your diet and exercising a little more and avoiding things that are bad for you make a person feel better. But it seems like almost everything is bad for you.

Look at the seafood announcements. One day it's, "Eat more squid," the next it's, "Please check your squid for mercury."

In the last few years, it seems researchers have decided the only safe things are water and tree bark, unless either one has been exposed to acid rain.

Red meat is bad for us; seafood is good, but it isn't properly inspected by the government so it may be contaminated.

Coffee and caffeine cause problems besides keeping us awake at night.

Sugar is dangerous, but artificial sweeteners can give you artificial diseases.

Ear more fruit and vegetables, but watch out for the pesticides on them

Practically everything causes cancer in white mice, but I think white mice cause cancer themselves.

Just about the only safe way to live, if you took each and every one of these pronouncements to heart, would be to stay inside a climate-controlled plastic bubble in which you can do jumping jacks and are fed only naturally grown roughage with absolutely no physical contact with anyone.

Personally, I think if people use their common sense and do things in moderation, the odds of any of these catastrophic calamities happening are less. Because, as they say, nobody gets out of this world alive, no matter how healthy they are.

CHAPTER 7
YARD ART

Whenever mankind looks upon an empty, vacant landscape, after admiring its appearance the very next consideration is how to improve it. This usually involves the addition of something, often something unnatural.

For vast fields, the improvements envisioned include trees, crops, parks, malls, condos and cities. On a smaller scale – the typical front lawn, for example – visions of ways to improve appearance include everything from trees and shrubs to painted tires and pink flamingos.

Somewhere deep in our psyche there must be a remnant of some ancient urge to decorate yards with lawn ornaments. Perhaps it stems from the day Og wandered by his buddy Ugh's cave and noticed the pink pterodactyl out front. He immediately decided he needed one. So, Og traipsed off to the nearest K-Cave, where he traded three rocks and 99 pieces of gravel, plus tax, for his own pink pterodactyl.

Over the eons, we continued to place various artifacts and decorations in front of our homes. Birdbaths have been popular yard ornaments, which also are functional. They provide a water source for birds and places for our fine-feathered friends to frolic. Some types are attractive and enhance a home's beauty. Others, however, couldn't enhance the appearance of an empty Fridigare box. Those usually are the ones found hidden in a corner of birdbath businesses.

Pink flamingos long have been favorite forms of yard art. For years, they were a must for all lawns. Gradually, the pink flamingo craze faded like the birds themselves in the summer sun, but in the past couple of years these plastic fowls have enjoyed a revival and slipped off the list of endangered species.

However, flamingos can be found in a series of shades other than pink. But, somehow, a purple flamingo or a blue flamingo just isn't the same as a pink one. There are just some traditions man wasn't meant to tamper with.

In the South, one of the traditional lawn decorations is a painted tire filled with dirt with a pink flamingo stuck in it. One also can find painted tires used as miniature flower gardens and shrub containers. The more creative decorators cut slits in the tire and pull the pointed pieces of rubber back to create a flower-like illusion.

A growing field of yard art consists of concrete critters. Many of these are painted to make them appear as life-like as concrete can be made to appear. These include brown and white Holsteins, chestnut mares and black and white Dalmatians.

One also can find pigs, sheep, ducks, chickens and other livestock preserved for posterity in cement.

My favorite concrete creature is one I saw just this past weekend. It was an ape, a concrete ape. A concrete ape slightly smaller than a Volkswagen, bent over with its hands dragging the ground and red reflectors for eyes.

Imagine, if you will, coming upon this stone simian some stormy night at the end of a driveway with its red eyes gleaming in the reflection of your headlights.

Kim wouldn't let me bring it home despite my position that with it we would likely never see another door-to-door insurance salesman again.

Oh, well, I guess I'll have to be satisfied with trees, shrubs and flowers when it comes to enhancing our yard's appearance, although I still think a concrete chimp could work wonders in satisfying primal decoration urges.

CHAPTER 8
IT'S THEM OR US

(The 1980s were a busy time for tax resistors such as the Posse Comitatus and conspiracy theorists, particularly in the Ozarks. After a few personal encounters with some of them, this was my response.)

"There's a conspiracy, you know. A worldwide conspiracy."

"What conspiracy?"

"You know, their conspiracy. They're out to get us."

"Who's 'they'?"

"You know. Them."

"Oh. Them, again. I thought they gave up."
"They never give up, and they never will, not until they control the world and everyone in it."

"Now, are they the ones who want to fluoridate the water, or are they the ones trying to control all the money?"

"Yes."

"Right."

"They also want to force us to pay taxes so children can get a free education, and we can have better roads and highways and get all kinds of services."

"Sounds pretty ominous to me."

"It is. And they want us to use paper for money instead of gold and silver."

"Well, I've got to admit gold ingots probably wouldn't fit into wallets very well."

"It's not funny. All that paper isn't worth a thing. You know, they took all the gold out of Fort Knox."

"Who did?"

"They did."

"Oh. What did they do with it?"

"I don't know, but I know they took it. I've got a pamphlet here that says they did."

"How do you know they didn't print the pamphlet to make you think they took all the gold out of Fort Knox?"

"Wait a minute, you may have something there."

"I was afraid of that."

"You know what else?"

"What?"

"They're replacing all the government's leaders with robots."

"They are?"

"Did you ever notice how blank-looking some of the people in Washington are?

"I thought that's how they always looked."

"No. Only robots look like that, their robots. Here, read this brochure. It explains everything.

"Everything?"

"Everything. It also tells how we can prevent their conspiracy from succeeding."

"How?"

"By not paying taxes."

"You mean like Al Capone and those other guys? They went to prison."

"They'll never send us to prison."

"Who's 'us'?"

"Us, the ones who are against Them."

"Oh."

"You see, if all of Us stick together, They can't possibly take over the world and turn everybody into robots and take away our gold and silver."

"You've got gold and silver?"

"No."

"Then how do you pay for things?"

"With my government pension check."

"Wait a minute, doesn't that come from tax money?"

"Not my taxes. I don't pay them."

"Oh, yeah."

"Well, I have to do what I believe in, and I don't think I should pay taxes, so I don't."

"What if everybody did that? How would you get your government pension check?"

"Don't confuse the issue."

"I'm sorry."

"You should be. After all, what we do will protect you, too."

"Who's we?"

"The Posse Comatose."

"What's the Posse Comatose?"

"Us."

"Right. How many people are in the Posse Comatose?"

"Everybody, except Them."

"What does the Posse Comatose do?"

"We all get together and complain about Them – and anybody else who doesn't agree with us – and don't pay taxes."

"Is it a violent group?"

"No, but we do have weapons to defend ourselves in case They come after us. And They will, you know."

"I hope not. What makes the Posse Comatose think it's right?"

"Because we are right. We're the only ones who are right and are obeying the law of the land. It's Them who are wrong."

"But, how do you really know you're right?"

"Well, if you keep it quiet so They don't find out … the Easter Bunny told me so."

"Right."

CHAPTER 9
IT'S THEM OR US, TAKE TWO

(This was a follow-up to the previous column and the response it generated.)

Some people just can't take a joke.

Not so long, in this very spot, there ran a piece entitled "It's Them or Us." Lately, I've been hearing from Us, or at least a few representatives of the Us faction.

As I said when I started my weekly ramblings, I rarely take the workings of the world seriously. And my purpose in this spot here is not to educate society about all the problems going on, but rather help folks escape them for the brief time it takes to read these words. Dwelling too much on problems we can't do anything about – or whose existence is doubtful – has the unfortunate side effect of reducing the mind to guacamole.

However, it would appear I hit a nerve with that particular column. Some folks have suggested I need to expand my education and learn about the dastardly activities of various cabals out to rule the world. Others have simply decided which "side" I'm on and declared they want nothing further to do with me. (Naturally, this hurt my feelings, and it took several seconds to get over the loss of their acquaintance.)

In the last few weeks, I've received more information than I ever wanted to know about the grand plans of Israel, people of color, the Rockefeller clan, the Trilateral Commission, the Council on Foreign Relations, international bankers, the Illuminati and others intent on taking over America and the world.

I think I should explain a few things.

First, if I want to read about nefarious conspiracies by zealous evil-minded groups, I'll read Robert Ludlum. At least his conspiracies are more credible than the one someone once told me about in which they alleged the Rockefeller family financed the Bolshevik Revolution against the Russian czar. Right, folks, one of the most capitalistic clans ever helped back the establishment of the most anti-capitalistic regime in history.

And if you believe that, I have some prime real estate to sell you in the Everglades.

Next, and this should have been clear in the earlier missive, I don't go along with the idea that there are secret and semi-secret groups out there just waiting for the right moment to pounce and become rulers of the world. There are some who believe that, and to be perfectly serious, some of them worry me more than the Rockefellers and the Trilateral Commission ever have.

However, they are free to believe whatever they want, and I don't care what they believe. I don't care if they want to get together and discuss plans about dealing with the CFR or Federal Reserve. I don't care if they want to stand on the street corner and espouse their beliefs.

I do care when they start contacting me in my own home and trying to convert me to their way of thinking. So, I'm willing to make a deal – I won't write columns in their living rooms if they'll leave me alone in mine.

Finally, I'm not writing about any specific individuals, although I'm sure some will realize they helped inspire this, and others might know the source of the inspiration. I don't want to hurt any particular person's feelings or start a running debate with anyone.

Like I said, I'm not particularly trying to enlighten anyone about anything, just lighten their cares for a few minutes once a week.

If some like it, I'm glad because that means I've done what I wanted to do. If others take offense, I'm sorry, but if it offends you, all you have to do is turn the page.

And that's no joke.

(Whatever happened to the Rockefeller family? They seem to have fallen off the conspiracy theorists' radar these days. Of course, now we have real conspirators such as al-Qaida to worry about.)

CHAPTER 10
TRISKAIDEKAPHOBES,
YOUR DAY HAS ARRIVED

All right class, listen up. Today we're going to learn a little about superstitions, particularly the ones involving triskaidekaphobia.

If the fact today is Friday the 13th causes you concern, anguish or panic, then you're a triskaidekaphobe. But that doesn't make you a bad person. Triskaidekaphobia is the fear of the number 13, and Friday the 13th is probably the most dreaded day for some people, next to April the 15th, which makes everyone depressed.

But for some people, it goes beyond Friday the 13th.

There are superstitions about Friday itself, and about 13. Together, they're enough to make some people hang a horseshoe, toss salt over their shoulders, seek out four-leaf clovers or cross their fingers.

Why are folks fearful of 13 in general, and Friday the 13th in particular?

It goes back many, many years, to ancient times, to before this old millennium was new. In those days, when folks had time on their hands after they finished herding their goats and camels, they sat around trying to figure out why they were spending their lives herding goats and camels while more fortunate people got to sit around eating dates and watching belly dancers. Finding no suitable explanation to their predicament, they decided they were the victims of bad luck.

While tabulating what caused their bad luck, these folks decided it must have had something to do with numbers because their number never seemed to come up.

Actually, seven, 12 and 40 were considered lucky numbers. They're found throughout ancient writings and even throughout the Bible. Twelve was considered particularly lucky and, for some reason, the number that followed it was considered evil. This was even before the Last Supper in the New Testament, which some folks consider as the origin of 13 as an unlucky number. But experts say it began even before that.

Even today 13 still is considered unlucky, although it's considered a blessing to be born on the 13th, and those who are will have good fortune, or so say some. But unlucky 13 is the norm.

Buildings avoid listing 13th floors, and hotels don't have Room 13, unless you check into the Bates Motel, where you can check out anytime you want but you can't leave. (No, wait, that's the Hotel California.)

And when Friday falls on the 13th, watch out. While most people celebrate Fridays -- TGIF and all that -- over the years it has been considered an unlucky day. (I just hope I haven't been unlucky enough to violate that restaurant chain's copyright.) Among the Friday superstitions:

- Don't start a new project on Friday or you'll never finish it. (Did the city street department start work on the square on a Friday?)
- Any ship that sails on Friday will have bad luck. (Just ask anyone who bought tickets on the Titanic.)
- Never start a trip on Friday or you'll meet with misfortune. (Try telling that to anyone who's survived Monday through Thursday and can't wait to hit the road.)
- Never start making a garment on a Friday unless you can finish it the same day, or you won't finish it. (Recycle street work crack above.)
- A bed changed on Friday will bring bad dreams. (Sorry, new parents, I didn't find anything about changing diapers on Fridays.)

While researching these superstitions, I ran across a few other superstitions that caught my attention.

- If you find a penny with the face up, pick it up. Face down, leave it on the ground. (Remember, if you pick it up the taxman gets half of it.)

- Catch a falling leaf in your hand and you will avoid a cold the following season. (Catch a falling tree and you will avoid a cold forever.)
- If you put your shirt on inside out, it means a bad day ahead. (If you put your pants on inside out, it means you had a wild night before.)
- If the bottom of your right foot itches, you are going to take a trip. (Or you're in need of foot powder.)
- Meeting a funeral procession is a sign of death. (So what's new?)
- Salty soup is a sign that the cook is in love. (More likely he's just not paying attention, which explains the creation of blackened catfish.)
- It is unlucky to look at the new moon over your left shoulder. (It is unlawful to moon someone over your left shoulder.)

So, after learning these odd little superstitions, triskaidekaphobes should feel better about themselves. Fearing 13 isn't nearly as ridiculous as some of these. But there may be hope for those who fear Friday the 13th.

To increase productivity and promote safety, the federal government is thinking of following an earlier precedent and moving all Fridays the 13th to Monday. After all, what's more frightening than a Monday, no matter what date it falls on.

CHAPTER 11
SIDE EFFECTS INCLUDE BAD TASTE, EMBARRASSMENT

E verybody's concerned about health these days. Wherever you turn there's always something there to remind you about taking care of yourself, eating right, getting the right medication, making sure you have enough health coverage and so on.

On television these health-related commercials often are sandwiched between the latest offering from McBurgee's (a three-quarter pound, four-cheese bacon-mayo burger with ranch dressing) and clothing ads featuring models who stopped growing at 12 and quit eating at 13.

I'm amazed at not only the number of health-related commercials, but also their varying subject matter. Sure, there are the old standbys such as spots for over-the-counter medication for headache relief, heartburn, gas, diarrhea and the heartbreak of psoriasis.

But now there are commercials for prescription medicines for each of these maladies as well as a host of others, some of which weren't even mentioned in mixed company let alone on TV 20 years ago.

I wasn't sure what to make of it the first time I saw Bob Dole talking about ... that problem and Bob Dole's own personal experience with it. Gee, Bob Dole, I don't think the campaign disclosure laws required you to go that far.

And take herpes, for example. A few years ago they wouldn't even talk about this on the news, now we're bombarded with commercials for medications to treat it. My favorite is the one with the people who don't have time to take the treatment -- although they had time to catch it -- but thanks to a supped-up version of the medicine they can be treated with one dose.

Hey, folks, I've got a better idea -- don't do anything to catch it in the first place!

One thing that really gets me is the list of potential side effects some of these medications might have. A couple of them have so many side effects it sounds as if they're still in the experimental stage. ("The lab rats refuse to take any more, so let's run some TV commercials and see if we can get anyone in the public to take it.")

Honestly, I think I'd rather put up with whatever's ailing me than take some of these medications. If I've got allergies, I'm not so sure it's that good a trade-off to take something that's going to give me dry mouth, headaches, nausea, insomnia, high blood pressure, abdominal cramps and curled toenails just to keep my nose from running.

Whatever happened to just going to the doctor with a problem and getting a prescription? What was wrong with that? Does getting Madison Avenue involved actually improve health care? Perhaps in one sense it does since we can now ask for specific medications that might be suitable for whatever problems we have. I just don't want to hear about some of these disorders and illnesses.

Speaking of medicine, health care and related subjects, I've run across a few thought-provoking items in my ramblings recently, and I offer them here for your consideration.

- When pills are to be taken in twos, why do they always come out of the bottle in threes?
- Some prescriptions say on the bottle, "Not for people with serious heart conditions." Is there such a thing as a non-serious heart condition?
- If instead of "sniffles" they were referred to as "'nasal leakage," would researchers be more serious about finding a cure for the common cold?
- Do people who eat nothing but natural foods ultimately die of natural causes?
- How do insomniacs know they're having trouble sleeping?
- Why is it you never hear of people who take nitro-glycerin exploding?

- If everybody around you gets a flu vaccination, would you need one?
- When people lose weight, where does it go?
- Should you tell a hypochondriac he looks terrible just to make him feel better?

CHAPTER 12
FILING FRIVOLOUS LAWSUITS IS HOT! HOT! HOT!

It's amazing what people will gripe about, and in the newspaper business you hear quite a few odd complaints every now and then.

Shoot, let's be honest -- we hear them every day. But our court system undoubtedly gets the oddest and most unusual complaints, things not even Robert Ripley would believe.

Every year people clog the courts with goofy complaints and suits. Most could be resolved if the complainants would just take responsibility for their own lives, not blame everything that happens to them as the result of someone else's actions or incompetence and accept the fact that every now and then any person is capable of doing things that make him look like a big doofus.

I know I've done my share, sometimes in print so that the whole world sees, and the bottom line has usually been it was my fault. I say when you have egg on your face, wipe it off and scramble it. (Yes, I know that doesn't quite have the ring of "when life hands you lemons, make lemonade," but it was the best I could do on the spur of the moment.)

Anyway, we live in a country where it seems as if there's a lawsuit filed every minute and potential plaintiffs lurk around every corner. Just ask any large corporation that deals with the public, like Wal-Mart, McDonalds or Coca-Cola.

For example, in Missouri a Blue Cross-Blue Shield employee sued IBM because she claimed the "faulty design" of its keyboards prevented her from working.

Or the New York woman who sued the manufacturer of The Clapper because she had to clap too hard to make her appliances work.

Or the California grocery store customer who sued because a six-pack of beer fell on her foot. She didn't sustain permanent damage or disability, but it hurt.

These kinds of complaints are almost as surreal as those filed by prison inmates, who admittedly have nothing better to do. A convict in Nevada sued because he got creamy peanut butter instead of chunky. In New York, an inmate claimed he lost sleep and suffered headaches and chest pains after receiving a defective haircut from an unqualified barber. Then there was the Oklahoma con who sued the state for violating his religious freedoms, but he couldn't say how because the main tenet of his religion was that its practices were secret.

Give me a break.

We can add an Arkansas case to this particularly excellent list. In Fayetteville, a city council member has filed a $1 million suit in federal court against W.H. Braum Inc. because, get this, his hot chocolate was too hot. Now, this might be a bit presumptive of me, but wouldn't logic dictate that when you order hot chocolate it might be a bit on the warm side? I mean that's why they call it "hot" chocolate.

The alderman and complainant in question, contends the small cup of hot chocolate he bought at a drive-through window fell out of the cup holder in his van. The contents of the small cup were so pyretic that the hot chocolate caused second-degree burns on his ankle and foot, melted the van's carpet and caused such intense pain that he couldn't use his brake and had to slam the van into reverse, then park, to stop.

Now that's hot chocolate. It's a good thing he didn't get an order of hot wings to go. They might have caused him to spontaneously combust.

He claims the hot chocolate was defective because it was ... hot. He thinks he's suffered $1 million worth of pain, medical costs and mental anguish, although I suspect by the time it's over he will have suffered far more mental anguish than dumping a cup of cocoa on his foot could ever cause.

If you think I'm taking this rather lightly, you're right. It's absurd, to be honest.

People wonder why the courts are the way they are these days. We've got way too many of these ridiculous litigations, unfortunately the courts, law-yers, government and businesses have to treat them seriously. In everyone of these cases, free world and prison alike, somebody has to answer the complaints, judges have to listen to them and, most importantly, somebody has to pay for them, often you, me and every other taxpayer and consumer.

In the end, the complainants usually wind up with far less than they seek, if they get anything.

And the rest of us wind up with lukewarm chocolate.

CHAPTER 13
MOTHERS MAKE THE WORLD GO AROUND

Where would we all be without mothers? They give us life, nurture us, raise us, help make us what we become.

That's part of why we have Mother's Day, that and the "why don't you ever call" guilt trip they can give us offspring. (The more cynical might say it's really a conspiracy of the greeting card, flower and candy industries whose commercials can really create feelings of guilt.)

All of us have special memories about our mothers and the things they've done for us. I know my Mom always has been there for me. Good times or bad, I've been able to count on her. She can't do much now, but she's still there for me.

I guess we all remember little things our mothers have done for us. I remember when I was in high school, sometimes I'd go home for lunch. My favorite that she made was hamburger steak with onions and homemade French fries. No one else could prepare it the way she could, and still can't.

Even after she and Dad moved here, I'd sometimes go over to their house for lunch and she'd fix that for me.

It was Mom who helped make me a reader and who made me a movie fan. Because Dad worked swing shift so much, Mom and I would watch movies on TV at night, catching the late show on Friday nights and staying up until Dad got home.

Mom always has liked Westerns and action movies and comedies and anything with John Wayne.

In a roundabout way, Mom got me interested in the news business. We'd watch the news every night -- she even became a fan of some local newscasters -- and there was hardly a news special we ever missed. We watched most of the space flight launches and breaking coverage of what are now historical events. That was before it was even feasible to fantasize about something like CNN. We had Chet Huntley and Walter Cronkite and Howard K. Smith in glorious black and white.

I guess it's those little things that really make you appreciate your mother, the things that come back in a flash of recollection when something jogs that part of your memory. Too often we take those little things for granted, not realizing how much of an effect they have on our lives.

So, what is a mother?

A mother is the one person you can go to with whatever problem you have and she'll make it better. Her advice may not always be what you want to hear, but she has your best interests at heart.

A mother knows that food can make anything easier. Hot homemade cookies and milk are a universal cure-all.

A mother can take the sting out of a boo-boo when nothing else will.

A mother is someone you can never hide anything from for long. Mothers have built-in lie detectors and can sense when something's wrong, even from across the country.

A mother is one person we can always depend on.

Happy Mother's Day, Mom, and to all the moms out there.

CHAPTER 14
ALL RIGHT, WHERE HAVE ALL THE FLOWERS GONE?

I've been pondering a few things lately.

For example, who did put the bop in the bop she bop, who put the ring in the ringa dinga ding dang?

Did anyone ever write an ending to the Lynyrd Skynyrd anthem "Freebird"? This song has been played constantly since its debut, without stop. Radio stations just play other songs around it, and the strains of this classic Southern rock song are traveling through space in one uninterrupted stream of radio waves.

It's said clothes make the man, but who makes the clothes?

How do you describe the taste of chicken to someone who has never eaten it?

If love is the answer, what's the question?

Where have all the cowboys gone, and whatever did happen to Randolph Scott?

Just when did politicians stop kissing babies and start chasing babes?

Is the disgusting stuff contestants eat on Fear Factor the real thing, or is the host just trying to psych them out with something that's really normal?

MTV is paying the Ozzy Osbourne family $5 million to follow them around and videotape their daily lives. Shoot, for just $2 million I'll shuffle around, cuss and look baffled at the world around me while being videotaped.

Did your mother ever tell you if you didn't stop making a face, your face would freeze in that position? Now, thanks to Botox, you can make your face freeze and look as astonished as Ozzy Osborne. And everybody thought botulism was bad for you.

Is there anyone in Mountain Home who removes dead animals from city streets? There has been a deceased possum, a hit-and-run victim, lying on College Street near one of its busiest intersections for at least four days. Of course, two more days and there won't be anything left to worry about.

How can George Lucas even come close to any kind of happy ending with his next *Star Wars* movie?

Why don't people get excited when Powerball has a $22 million jackpot? Why do they wait until it's $80 million and everyone else is buying tickets?

If you wear sunglasses at your desk, no one can tell you're sleeping. Unless you snore.

Why do some restaurants make you walk through the smoking section to get to the non-smoking section?

Why is it everyone is driving faster than the speed limit -- except the car in front of me?

Is there something difficult to understand about the words "enter" and "exit" above doors, or does it just really not matter to some people? And if it doesn't, why bother designating entrances and exits?

What's Edna going to do without Earl in those furniture commercials?

Could it be too late to stop cloning? Just listen to Britney, Christina and J Lo. And are Al Pacino, Dustin Hoffman and Robert De Niro really interchangeable?

Would western civilization collapse if Joe Estevez -- Martin Sheen's brother -- and Frank Stallone -- Sylvester Stallone's brother -- made a movie together, or just the company making the movie?

Who did write the book of love?

And, perhaps the most important thing I've pondered in the last five minutes, how do they get a full glass of milk into every slice of Kraft Singles?

CHAPTER 15
HOW TO TELL YOU'RE
SPEEDING IN THE FAST LANE

What hectic, fast-paced times we live in these days. For all the alleged leisure time people are supposed to have it seems most folks hardly have a chance to keep up with anything.It's as if somebody switched the speed of the world from 33 1/3 rpm to 78 rpm. (You youngsters can ask parents or grandparents what that means.) I suspect if you added up all the things people need to do in a day a lot of people would find it totals 36 hours.

Get up, get to school, get to work. Work, work, work. Throw in a couple of meetings. Get the children at school. Get them to their extracurricular activities. (This is especially fun for those parents with three children whose ages are in close proximity of one another so that in the space of an hour they have to be in three different places, each at the farthest edge of town.)

Get home, take care of chores, make sure you've picked up the youngsters, take them back

out for their games, meetings and anything else they need to do. Go grocery shopping, go to Wal-Mart, go to the post office, go back to Wal-Mart to pick up what you forgot the first time, go to your next meeting, stop for gasoline, go back to Wal-Mart for what you forgot the second time you were there. Go home, get the children ready for bed, check the e-mail, read the regular mail, catch five minutes of TV, put the children to bed, hit the showers, go to bed. Get up, get to school, get to work ...

And so on.

If those aren't enough indications that your life's moving faster than a rocket car on the Bonneville Salt Flats, here are a few more signs that you're getting too much of modern life.

- You try to enter your PIN number on the microwave.
- You haven't played solitaire with real cards for years.
- You have a list of 15 phone numbers to reach your family of three.
- Your idea of organization is multiple, color-coded Post-It notes.
- Your reason for not staying in touch with friends is they're not online.
- When you make phone calls from home, you automatically dial "0" to get an outside line.
- Free food left over from meetings is a key part of your staple diet.
- You've just been given an assignment, and it's already late.

- If you're female, you only have makeup for fluorescent lighting.
- Being sick is defined as you can't walk or you're in the hospital.
- Your relatives and friends describe your job as "works with computers."
- The most current photo your family has of you is on a milk carton.
- You chat several times a day with a stranger from South America, but you haven't spoken to your next-door neighbor in a year.
- You e-mail your buddy at work -- who sits at the desk next to you -- to ask: "Do you want to get a Coke?" And he sends you an e-mail replying: "Yeah, give me five minutes."
- You hear most of your jokes via e-mail rather than in person.
- When you go home after a long day at work you still answer the phone with the name of your business.
- You know exactly how many days you've got left until you retire.

CHAPTER 16
REDNECK ETIQUETTE FROM MARTHA STEWART

(This was written before Martha Stewart went to prison.)

Poor Martha Stewart.

America's wealthiest home economics instructor has been beset by so many woes in recent times, from an infamous stock scandal to being portrayed by Cybil Shepard in a TV movie.

She still has her television show where she offers interesting tips on such things as how to make a meat loaf sandwich and turning horse apples into decorative table settings. To say she's fallen on hard times might be a bit extreme, especially if she landed on her bank account. But Martha has seen some of the sheen come off her image.

So it wasn't surprising to learn that circulating on the Internet, which is known for its accuracy and reliability, new Martha Stewart tips especially for those of the redneck persuasion. Now, I'm not sure how Jeff Foxworthy is taking to this infringement on his territory. In fact, some of the alleged Martha Stewart tips for rednecks might actually have originated with the comic who made being a redneck chic.

Anyway, not too long ago, I received an e-mail featuring Martha Stewart's tips for rednecks. I won't vouch for their accuracy, but I thought a few of them were worthy of sharing and decided to add a few of my own.

For example, Martha says (or "sez." if you prefer):

- It's tacky to take a beer cooler to church, even if there is a softball game after services.
- It's rude to shoot at people in your front yard without first identifying them.
- It is considered polite to offer to share your Copenhagen or Skoal with your date. It is considered impolite to ask for a smooch while you still have a dip between your lip and gum.
- Do not burn rubber while driving in a funeral procession, especially if you're driving the hearse.
- At a four-way stop, the vehicle with the biggest tires has the right of way.
- Always offer to bait your date's hook, especially on the first date.
- When entertaining in your house, the guest gets first opportunity to lick the serving spoon.

- Do not let the dog eat from the table, no matter how good his manners are.
- Livestock is not considered an appropriate wedding gift.
- It is poor form at a wedding to ask the bride out on a date.
- A six-pack and a Moon Pie does not qualify as a six-course meal and dessert.
- Vienna sausage is not a food group.
- Clipping your toenails at the dinner table is inappropriate. Biting your toenails anywhere is inexcusable. Biting someone else's toenails is just plan weird.
- No matter what, do not clean deer in the living room, even if you promise to spread out newspapers on the floor.
- Leaving car parts in the kitchen sink is not a good idea. However, car parts on coffee tables do make interesting conversation pieces.
- Velvet paintings of Elvis, The Last Supper, Dale Earnhardt or of animals playing poker can turn any trailer into a showplace, especially if lit with a blacklight.

And, finally,:

- Duct tape can be used to solve any decorating problem.

Thought for the Week: "Man cannot live by bread alone. That's why there's bologna."

CHAPTER 17
LIFE AT THE WHEEL: A LITTLE DRIVING MUSIC

Ｐeople think of their vehicles as something more than mere transportation.

They're our sanctuary, an extension of ourselves, our home away from home. We love our cars and trucks and SUVs, and love being in them.

I was thinking that while rearranging the accumulation of sacks I've acquired in my truck. Between my seats, I've stashed plastic bags from various stores, mainly because I put the purchases that were once in them to use immediately or slide the contents into my briefcase.

A plastic bag is like duct tape. You never know when it'll come in handy.

Anyway, it's amazing how people feel about their vehicles. Many people pamper them, keeping them showroom neat by washing and vacuuming them, waxing and polishing them, treating them better than their spouses.

Another thing some do to preserve their vehicle's appearance is to straddle the line between parking spaces, thus taking up two spots to leave plenty of space between them and anyone else needing to park. That way no one can bump the car with their car doors.

Don't you just hate it when somebody does that, especially in a lot where parking space is at a premium? It sort of falls into the category of folks who aren't handicapped parking in a handicap space.

Then there are the things that people do while their vehicles are in motion. Some folks must have automatic pilot instead of cruise control. They seem too occupied with other things to be driving.

I was navigating my way along Highway 62 the other day when a car pulled up beside me. The driver was smoking a cigarette, talking on a cell phone, drinking a cup of coffee and trying to hold onto the wheel, all at once...

At least he wasn't putting on makeup, too.

Trying to do so many things can be dangerous when driving. Especially in an area like ours where, for whatever reason, there seem to be so many automotively challenged drivers.

Apparently people think they can do whatever they want once they're in their vehicles and that no one can see them. How else can you account for those folks stopped at traffic lights with fingers up their noses? Or picking at their teeth.

Actually, some people perform complete dental self-examinations in the rear view mirror at red lights.

A VIEW FROM THE HILLS

Many of us work on our musical talent behind the wheel. I've been known to play air guitar, steering wheel percussion and dash keyboards while waiting for a traffic light to change. I like having a little driving music when I'm behind the wheel. A little Bob Seeger, George Thorogood, some Rolling Stones provides good background music for driving.

Sometimes you can tell what people are listening to in other vehicles.

A person performing a drum solo on the steering wheel obviously is listening to rock, maybe even an oldies station that's playing Wipeout. Someone whose head is bouncing back and forth and who appears to be having convulsions is listening to heavy metal.

A driver keeping time with the music, whether by tapping the steering wheel or slowly nodding his head, probably is listening to a country station. A motorist whose head is swaying may be enjoying easy listening, or perhaps even light classics.

If your vehicle is vibrating, the fuzzy dice on your mirror is shaking and your ear drums are near collapse, the car next to you actually is a bass speaker on wheels, the driver has the volume at full blast, and it doesn't matter what he's listening to because he has to be deaf.

CHAPTER 18
WHEN ALL ELSE FAILS, DUCT TAPE KEEPS US TOGETHER

D o you ever get the feeling that the world's falling apart? That things just aren't holding together very well? That there has to be something to pull everything in concert again?

Well, there is something that can do just that. To many it's almost magical, if not mystical. It's the ultimate solution to many problems, and something no one should be without.

What is this wondrous miracle producer?

Duct tape.

That's right, duct tape.

No matter what size or color it is, duct tape may be the ultimate solution to many of the world's problems. With duct tape, you can fix virtually anything, no matter how big or small it may be. Duct tape is the perfect tool whether you're a handy man or all thumbs. Remember the immortal words of Red Green, PBS' duct tape guru, "If the women don't find you handsome, at least be handy." There are no batteries or electrical connections required for duct tape, it doesn't use any fuel, and you can't smash your thumb with it or cut yourself on it. It requires minimal training, and anyone can use it, from 4 to 100 and every age in between.

Duct tape has been around as long as I can remember. I think there may have been some references to duct tape in a couple of World War II era movies I've seen, so it has been in use quite a while, probably at least 60 years or so. (I wouldn't be surprised if someone found a B-17 that's been in a jungle somewhere since the end of the war with duct tape that was put on a wing in 1944 still holding it in place.)

I know I swear by duct tape. Eli definitely is a believer in the power of duct tape, as are most Scouts and Scouters I know. Carpenters, electricians, plumbers, mechanics, do-it-yourselfers all appreciate duct tape. Campers, hunter, anglers also know the value of duct tape.

What is the fascination with this traditionally silver-colored sticky wonder of the world? For one thing, it's versatile, sort of the Swiss Army Knife of tapes. As I mentioned, it can be used to fix virtually anything. Why, I bet MacGyver could even make a kayak out of duct tape and twigs.

Here are just a few potential uses for duct tape:

- It can bind objects together, such as pipes, poles, sticks, stakes. It works on plastic, metal, wood.
- It can hold wires together, whether you're putting them in a bundle or splicing them.

- You can wrap enough around a pipe or a hose to help seal leaks.
- It can be used to label ice chests, tool boxes, tackle boxes, backpacks, luggage, packages, jackets, individual tools, your children's clothes, Aunt Edna's plate collection, Uncle Harvey's dental plates, etc., etc.
- It can be used to patch tents, tarps, your pants, that hole in your pocket, your favorite cap, your shoes, Uncle Harvey's dental plates, Aunt Edna's plate collection, the kitchen curtains, sleeping bags, sheets, blankets, the hammock you wind up sleeping in after patching the wife's kitchen curtains, etc., etc.
- You can use it like moleskin to prevent or protect blisters on your feet, whichever comes first.
- In an emergency, it makes a handy substitute for sutures and can hold a bandage in place.
- You can repair the frames on your glasses. In a pinch, you can even make sunglasses with duct tape and a pinhole.
- You can do body work on vehicles by covering holes or rust spots. It can seal cracks in tail light covers, hold exhaust pipes in place and, with enough, you could probably put a bumper back on your truck. You could use it for a bumper sticker (see label uses above).
- It can remove unwanted body hair.

- You can cover unattractive wiring with it, especially wiring that crosses the floor and could present a safety hazard.
- It can be used to wrap gifts (and it makes an excellent stocking stuffer).

Yes, duct tape is a modern marvel, something no household, workshop, office or school should be without and that should be kept in every car, truck, SUV, RV, boat, canoe and aircraft. You never know when you may need it.

Actually, I think something I ran across while surfing the Internet best sums up the essence of duct tape:

"Duct tape is like The Force -- it has a light side, a dark side and it holds the universe together."

CHAPTER 19
TO SLEEP, PERCHANCE TO DREAM, OR SNORE

There are times I think I could get into this hibernation thing pretty easily.

Through much of my life, I've been a night owl. Staying up late was never a big deal for me, and the advent of 24-hour satellite television didn't deter my nocturnal ways. Of course, there are times when you have a couple of hundred television channels at your fingertips and nothing to watch, even at 1 in the morning.

In college, I could stay up until the wee hours, get a couple hours of sleep then make it to a day of classes with no problem. Even when I got into the real world, I could keep late hours and still seem unaffected by it.

Once, when I was working in Texarkana, several associates and I stayed up all night one Friday. Somewhere along the way, I got my second wind and shortly after dawn on Saturday I was on the road to Canton Trade Days at Canton, Texas, about a hundred miles away. (Trade Days is one of the biggest flea markets/yard sales/kitsch collections you've ever seen.)

Naturally, I was considerably younger then, that age when you can get away with a lot more physically. In your 20s, it seems you can overindulge and over-imbibe and recover quickly. Now it takes longer to recuperate, and that makes such activities hardly worth it.

That was then.

These days I'm still somewhat of a night owl on occasion. But there are times when I sit down on the couch that I'm out faster than Dagwood. I think it's the couch's fault. There's something about it that induces drowsiness. Whether I'm reading or watching TV or drawing, if I'm sitting on the couch, it's not long before I'm inspecting the back of my eyelids.

Of course, whenever Kim asks me if I'm awake I always answer affirmatively. That's usually followed with, "Then why were you snoring?"

How do you explain making a snoring sound if you were awake? I usually just deny it. Until the next time she asks me if I'm awake, about five minutes later.

There are other times the old sandman gives me a tap, such as sitting under a tree in the sunshine while deer hunting or watching a boring movie. Actually, there are times when it seems I could nod off to sleep in nothing flat.

But I still maintain that just because my eyes are closed doesn't mean I'm asleep. Sometimes I concentrate better with my eyes closed, get a better mental image of what I'm listening to by focusing with my ears instead of my eyes.

At concerts, for example. It's amazing how better focused I am on the music with my eyes closed. Sitting at my desk, trying to come up with a column idea, the thought process just works so much better with my eyes closed.

And I figure that as long as I'm not snoring then I'm not asleep, especially since I'm still aware of what's going on around me.

At least that's my story, and I'm sticking to it.

CHAPTER 20
IS IT JUST ME, OR DO YOU FEEL A DRAFT? IT'S ME

Did you ever have the feeling that something isn't quite right?

You can't put your finger on it, but you know something is amiss. Something potentially embarrassing.

That's what happened to me today (or, yesterday, by the time you read this, or Friday, to follow proper AP style).

Earlier in the morning, I'd noticed a seam in my trousers was giving way. It was one that recently had been repaired. At that point there really wasn't a problem. It was where no one would notice even if it came apart.

Ah, little did I suspect ...

I went to a lunch meeting, and as I sat there, it felt a little cool where I sat. Or, perhaps I should say what I was sitting on felt cool. And I don't mean the chair.

Anyway, when lunch was finished, and I went to my truck, things still felt a little nippy around the nether regions. Reaching behind me, I didn't feel anything that seemed out of place.

I drove to Wal-Mart wanting to check on a couple of things. As I walked across the parking lot, things still didn't seem right. It was one of those times when having eyes in the back of your head would have come in handy.

Once inside the store, I really felt as though I needed to check further, so I stopped by their public facility. I realize this is a bit personal, but, in current vernacular, I dropped trou.

I could see the floor through the seat of my pants.

Needless to say, this presented a dilemma. First, I wasn't too sure how long I'd been going around with, how can I put this delicately, part of my derriere on display.

Have you ever noticed people won't tell you if your derriere is on display? You stroll around, feeling every breeze, and no one will tell you where it's coming from. However, I can see how some people might take offense to being told their seat's hanging out, no matter how badly they needed to be told.

Of course, judging by some recent fashion trends, letting your rear end and assorted other anatomical parts hang out is the in thing. However, my figure's not compatible with such trends. (When I got the tux for my wedding in 1980, the clerk noted on the receipt "built like a fireplug." Things haven't changed, other than now I'm built more like a water tank.)

Anyway, the discovery of the Northwest Passage through the seat of my pants presented a problem. I couldn't spend the rest of the day subjecting the world to my southerly view. So, trying to be as cool as possible -- and trying not to bend over -- I went in search of another pair of pants.

The particular size I needed was somewhat scarce. I'm a size-square kind of guy, and that size either isn't stocked in quantity or sells quickly. I also noticed sizes in that range were all on the bottom of the shelves, which required squatting to go through them rather than bending over and subjecting other customers to an early moonrise.

There were plenty of jeans and pants for people who are waistline deprived, and I found two in which an entire family of gypsies could have lived. Things weren't looking real good until, finally, I found them, a pair of pants just my size.

Changing pants in a public facility isn't as dignified as it sounds, especially when you've just bought them. Now I know how a shoplifter must feel, except I had a receipt, all the stickers and a pair of pants that could double as a pullover stuffed in the sack when I left.

Fortunately, the remainder of the day wasn't as eventful as that, although I did learn one valuable lesson from this that I'd like to pass along. Always remember: Friends don't let friends walk around with their derrieres displayed.

CHAPTER 21
A FEW OF LIFE'S
LITTLE WONDERS

This has been one of those weeks that make you sit down and wonder about what's going on in the world and why some things are the way they are.

For instance, did you ever wonder why radio stations have color weather radar? Wouldn't black and white do? I mean, their listeners can't see it, and they've got to take the disc jockey's word for what it shows.

And you better hope the disc jockey's not color blind, otherwise that light rain he says is coming cold turn out to be the worst thunderstorm since Noah invented the boat-building business.

Why do fast-food places and other businesses have hot-air hand driers in their restrooms for sanitary reasons and hospitals don't? The little labels on the driers say they're supposed to be more sanitary than paper towels, yet practically every hospital I've been in has paper towels in all their restrooms. It seems if the hot air driers are so sanitary then hospitals would use them.

Of course, I've never found a hot-air drier – or, more accurately, a lukewarm-air drier – that gets your hands dry. You stand there looking like the villain in a silent movie as you rub your wet hands together under lukewarm air, and when the drier stops you're still standing there rubbing your wet hands together. Graffiti artists have altered the instructions on most hot-air driers I've seen, and the revised instructions usually work better, although instead of having wet hands you wind up with damp pants from rubbing your hands on them.

Did you ever notice how many people don't know how to read Entrance and Exit signs? I don't know how many times I've gone to a store and watched people using the exit doors for entrances and the entrances as exits. And they usually go the wrong way at the most inconvenient times, such as when you've got an armload of packages and are standing within range of the door. These folks come barreling through just in time to hit you with the door.

Along those same lines, it amazes me how many people can't read the signs that designate an area as a fire lane and apparently don't realize that a yellow curb and yellow stripes mean they shouldn't park there. At one local store, there's always several cars parked beside the yellow curb marking the fire land in front of the business.

The ones who can't find a space to park in along the fire lane generally pick their second choice for parking spots – the area at the end of a parking row which has yellow stripes that designate it as a no-parking area. Usually these are the second-closest spots to the store, with the closest being the fire lane. This usually results in obstructed traffic and generally creates problems for those looking for legitimate parking spaces who sometimes question the legitimate origins of those in the no-parking spaces.

Did you ever wonder where those tabloid papers get their stories? We get AP's wire service and a couple of other news services here at Sixth and Hickory, and I've never seen any of them carrying stories about a 70-year-old woman giving birth to quintuplets in a refrigerator during an earthquake. Of course, many of the events recorded in those slightly yellow pages have a dateline of South Turban, India or Oak Park, Mongolia. That make the stories a little hard to verify, and makes me wonder how they found out about them in the first place.

These are just a few of the things I've wondered about lately. With any luck, maybe next week will be a little busier, and I won't have to wonder about so much about what I'll do for a column.

CHAPTER 22
ADULT EDUCATION

I'm all for people expanding their horizons and learning new things through community college programs, but a course called "The Art of High Heels" may be stretching matters a bit.

Now, I come up with some strange items every now and then, but not even I could think up a course with such a title. This is genuine. It's one of many listed in a little booklet we got in the mail this week at Sixth and Hickory from one of our state universities. The course is part of an adult education program, also known as continuing education, the school offers and, ostensibly, appears to be some sort of physical education course. Still, it sounds rather kinky to me.

There are other equally interesting courses among those listed. For example, there's one on being an executive wife aimed at women who want to assist their husbands' careers. At $200 for the two-session course, it had better help somebody's career besides the instructor's.

Then there's the beauty pageant preparation course for $100 in which young ladies can learn how to smile continuously for three days in a driving blue norther while maintaining their poise and grace.

For $150, you can learn how to get your closet in order through a private consultation in your very own home. I suppose using a janitor's closet on campus wouldn't be as effective.

The school also offers courses in Middle Eastern dance and intermediate Arabic, either of which could come in handy if you should find yourself somewhere in the Sinai.

I've noticed over the years that colleges offer a variety of what they call noncredit courses through community programs. In addition to expanding one's mind, such courses also give you a chance to get out of the house for a night or two. But there always seems to be something lacking in these programs, and I've tried to come up with some classes that might interest potential students.

- Doublespeak 503. It will help individuals understand what politicians are saying during the year's elections and interpret their statements accordingly. For example: Students will hear speeches by such luminaries as Eddie Bethune, Davy Pryor, Ronnie Reagan and Walt Mondale and then be required to convince their fellow class members that none favor tax increases.

- Electrical Engineering 527. In this class, students will be required to rewire the entire rate structure of Middle South Utilities so Arkansas does not receive any further shocks from the Grand Gulf power plant. The registration fee will be determined by the FERC.

- Alchemy .999. With this course, students will examine the ancient art of turning things into precious metals. The final exam will be to change the national monetary standard to silver and gold.

- Offensive Driving. Every day it becomes more hazardous to venture forth on the highway. In this class, students will learn skills necessary for traveling the streets of Mountain Home, including lane changing without warning, ignoring traffic signals, how to honk horns the instant a stop light changes and, most important, how to go the wrong way around the square.

- Clerk abuse 599. This course provides instruction in methods of being rude to store clerks in order to achieve maximum satisfaction. Included will be lessons on how to properly throw money on the counter, how to complain about prices to those who have no say in price setting, how to insult a clerk's entire family lineage and how to hold up a line by picking

87

out only those items without price stickers. A prerequisite to this course is that no one may have taken any lessons in good manners.\

CHAPTER 23
A MORNING TO REMEMBER

"**O**bviously a major malfunction."

That comment may be one of the greatest understatements of all time. It was uttered by Mission Control seconds after space shuttle Challenger burst into an orange ball of flames in the azure Florida sky Tuesday morning in front of the families of her crew and thousands of television viewers.

The voice was calm, as Mission Control's voice always is. No matter what the situation, those who head into the last frontier can rest assured that the quiet tones of Mission Control will be there as it has been since Americans first ventured past the atmosphere.

And that same voice has assured us with our feet firmly planted on the ground that all will be well for the courageous few who go where none of us may ever travel.

But Tuesday morning, a morning to remember, not even Mission Control could give comfort as we watched seven people perish on national television.

Over and over again, we were shown what happened 75 seconds after Challenger took to the skies above Cape Canaveral.

Ever since man first began exploring space, we have been awed by the achievements of those who flew into space, first in the tiny Mercury capsules, and now aboard the first true spaceships. I recall many a morning as a child when I'd rise to see those with the right stuff ride their rockets into space. Sitting there in the comfort of our living room, my mother and I could hardly believe someone was actually going into space. Except for those flights launched after the morning school bell, there was hardly a mission I didn't watch take off for the unknown.

On a Sunday afternoon in July of 1969, watching a scratchy black-and-white picture on a portable TV, I was amazed to see Neil Armstrong put the first footprints on the moon. It was Buck Rogers and Flash Gordon come alive. Less than a year later, Apollo 13 – unlucky 13 – reminded us of the dangers of space exploration. When it returned from its near-tragic flight to the moon, we all breathed a sigh of relief.

Then, when we stopped sending men to the moon, people didn't seem as excited about the space program. When space flights began, we knew the seven Mercury astronauts – Alan Shepard, John Glenn, Gus Grissom, Gordon Cooper, Deke Slayton, Wally Schirra and Scott

Carpenter. But as the space program progressed, few could name those who followed them.

Oh, interest revived when the shuttles began flying, but it didn't seem as strong as it had during those first flights and the lunar missions. Space flights were becoming almost commonplace, so much so that the Big Three television networks rarely took time out for live coverage of the launches. Rather than being the lead story on the evening news, shuttle launches slipped to the spots after the first or second commercial breaks. The Big Three hadn't bothered to cover Tuesday's launch live, although CNN was there, as it usually is at such events, to show what's happening as it happens.

There was high interest in Challenger's mission since Christa McAuliffe, a New Hampshire schoolteacher who was a schoolgirl herself when man first journeyed into space, was the first civilian to go aboard a shuttle mission. She planned to deliver a lesson from space later in the week, so school children around the country were watching the history-making launch. But, instead of a bright spot in the history of space flight, Mrs. McAuliffe and the six other crewmembers will be remembered on pages edged in black.

I was at Baker's Drug, sipping a cup of coffee and visiting with Pappy Miles, when the news came over the radio. Those of us in the drug store listened anxiously as the reports were updated. Then I returned to the office here at Sixth and Hickory, where the television in the editor's office already was tuned to CNN, which was showing a replay of the first – and final – seconds of the 25th shuttle mission.

It's amazing how something so tragic, so far away from here, could touch us so deeply. None of use here knew those aboard Challenger, but everyone felt for their families who watched them leave on a flight that would never return, felt for the 11 children who would never see one of their parents again.

We hear of tragedies with greater loss of life and see pictures of the aftermath and are touched by it. But in this case, we saw the tragedy as tit happened, and that cut much deeper, making it feel a little more personal.

It's unlikely we'll forget Challenger's ill-fated flight, or the courage of those aboard who have slipped the surly bonds of Earth to touch the face of God.

CHAPTER 24
OFF (AND ON) THE TOP
OF MY HEAD

I've always been partial to hats, and since the new picture started running with this column I've had quite a few comments about my fedora.

Most people who have said anything like the Beaver Hats DeLuxe that I bought at Sam Swartz Men's store in Greenville, Texas in 1974, which means I had my fedora when Indiana Jones was just a gleam in Steven Spielberg's imagination.

It replaced both a straw hat and a cheaper gray felt fedora I had worn. The straw had seen better days, and the felt hat just wasn't the same after a night in Dallas when I was still young and foolish.

I've been a hat fancier most of my life. Pictures my parents made on my second birthday show me wearing one of those straw cowboy hats made specifically for little buckaroos who aren't old enough for the real thing. Being from Texas, and a Western fan to boot, cowboy hats figured prominently in my boyhood wardrobe. I even had a couple of LBJ hats like the ones worn by LBJ and my Uncle Ben.

When I wasn't wearing a hat, I wore caps, and I still do. I had a succession of baseball and baseball-type caps over the years. One of my favorites was an orange flight deck cap with the number of the aircraft carrier my cousin served on in the Navy.

To me, hats are more practical than going bare-headed. They keep the sun out of your eyes and shade your face. They keep rain and snow off your head as well as helping keep you warm. People have always told me I'd go bald if I kept wearing hats. While things are getting a little thin on top, I figure if I'm wearing a hat nobody will know if I'm bald or not.

Hats can give a person character. They can make you look distinguished, daring, debonair and distinctive. They stick in people's memories and, thus, make you stand out in heir minds, to. I don't think a wardrobe would be complete without at least one hat.

A hat has a character all its own, and it can add to its wearer's character as well. No one can think of Humphrey Bogart without his snap-brim fedora and trench coat. Imagine John Wayne, and you'll likely picture him in his Stetson. And, yes, how could anyone think of Harrison Ford without seeing an image of Indiana Jones wearing his well-worn hat?

Of course, its true that no everyone can wear hats well. I've seen a few folks wearing cowboy hats who were a couple of gallons shy of filling out their 10-gallon chapeaus. Then there are those people who look like inverted mushrooms in any type of headgear.

Folks have worn hats for a lot more years than they haven't. Hats fell out of grace when JFK was president and didn't wear them. However, hats have been making a comeback in the last few years, which is fortunate for us true believers who have worn hats even when we got funny looks from people.

An off-white Stetson, a gray felt Resistol, a straw Resistol and a straw cowboy hat made in Mexico have occupied my closet and my head in more recent years. I also have a well-worn Panama – not the planter's hat some folks pawn off as a Panama hat – that used to be white, and another straw chapeau from last summer's vacation.

And that doesn't account for various gimme caps and ball caps I alternate wearing, and which Kim probably would give to the nearest charity that would cart them off.

But no matter. As long as I've got a place to hang it, I'll be wearing my hats.

I still have my Sam Swartz hat, although it has been retired. I still have several hats and caps that I wear, especially since I'm thinner on top than I was when I first wrote this.

CHAPTER 25
SAYING WHAT YOU MEAN

Strother Martin uttered one of my favorite movie lines when, addressing Paul Newman and a chain gang in "Cool Hand Luke," he explained, "What we have here … is failure to communicate."

Sometimes folks fail to communicate just what they mean, and the results can occasionally be amusing. There are the accident reports in which those involved describe slightly unusual circumstances that contributed to their mishaps. "The elderly gentleman was crossing against the light, so I ran over him," was one such description of an accident.

In another report, the accident victim told the officer, "I was driving along the road when this telephone pole collided with my car." A third example of failing to communicate was, "I looked at my mother-in-law and proceeded to drive over a cliff."

Stopped for speeding, one motorist explained to the officer "I just washed my hair and was trying to get it dry." Another speeder told the patrolman who stopped him, "I needed to go to the bathroom and was hurrying to the next service station."

A little item along those likes came across my desk this week. A note on it said it was from the University of Pittsburgh and contained samples of unclear writing taken from actual letters received by a welfare department in applications for support. While the meaning can become clear after a couple of readings – and the samples were not a putdown of anyone – an initial reading can make one pause to ponder the unusual forces at work in the writers' lives.

For example, one writer said, "You have changed my little boy to a girl. Will this make any difference?" It might to the child, but probably not to the welfare department. Along those lines, a woman wrote that, "I have no children as yet as my husband is a truck driver and works day and night." No one apparently knew exactly what kind of help she wanted.

Another woman apparently got the help she needed, but there was a failure to communicate somewhere along the line. "In accordance with your instructions, I have given birth to twins in the enclosed envelope."

Having children appears to have played a large part in the lives of the letter writers. "In answer to your letter, I have given birth to a boy weighing 10 pounds," wrote one individual. "I hope this is satisfactory."

"I am writing the welfare department to say that my baby was born two years old," said another writer. "When do I get my money?"

"This is my eighth child. What are you going to do about it?" inquired another mother.

Then there was the letter writer who said, "I cannot get sick pay. I have six children. Can you tell me why?"

One woman seemed to express mixed emotions in her letter. "I am glad to report that my husband who is missing is dead." It's not known if the same woman wrote again, but another letter asked, "Please find out for certain if my husband is dead. The man I am now living with can't eat or do anything until he knows." One wonders if the gentleman was concerned, or simply worried that the husband might return.

Another correspondent appeared to have overcome the problem of death. "Unless I get my husband's money pretty soon, I will be forced to live an immortal life."

I wonder if Strother Martin ever got letters like that?

CHAPTER 26
CONSUMER EVOLUTION

While taking time out for breakfast at a lo-cal fast-food restaurant the other morn-ing, I kept noticing that the drive-up window was a pretty busy place. Throughout the entire time I was there, it seemed there was a con-stant stream of car-bound customers ordering their food to go.

As I studied this phenomenon, I thought back to a story I'd read from the wire service. It dealt with an exhibit of 50 things that revolutionized life for the consumer. A wide-range of objects was included on the list, including antibiotics, laundry detergent, automatic washing machines, power mowers, re-frigerators, fast-food restaurants, Scotch tape, tele-vision, VCRs, personal computers, stereos, Volkswagens and credit cards.

While antibiotics ranked first, the credit cards might be the most important since they could be sued to pay for all the other items on the list. Of course, they also can be blamed for sending us all into debt trying to get as many of the other items

101

listed as possible. After, all, some folks think as long as they have plastic they don't need money, especially if they could use one credit card to pay the bills they owe on another card.

Now, the story I read didn't name all 50 items on the list, so I'm not sure what else might have been included. But as I watched the folks pulling up to the drive-in window, I thought surely that needed to be one of them. I don't know when the drive-in window was first introduced, but it certainly has changed the way we do some of our business.

Thanks to the drive-in window, we never have to leave our cars to make deposits and withdrawals at the bank, to pay bills and, if there's any money left over, to get a bite to eat at a fast-food place. In some places, the drive-in window, or more accurately the drive-through window – which should not be taken literally – is even being used for worshipping, funeral visitations and pawning items to pay the credit card bills.

Sipping my coffee, I tried to think of other things that have changed our lives that should be on the Top 50 list.

Styrofoam (registered trademark) cups, like the one I was drinking from, have made changes in our lives. Now when we're done drinking something on the go, we can toss the cup away and not have to worry about washing it.

Aluminum cans have enabled everyone to be macho. Even Eli, with the right grip, can now mash a can, a feat once reserved only for muscle men trying to impress the ladies and intimidate rivals. It's hard to be impressive and intimidating when you do something a 19-month-old boy can do.

Childproof caps on bottles certainly have changed things. If you don't have a child, you can't get into the blasted things half the time.

Microwave ovens certainly have brought about great changes. Now we can burn a roast in half the time and turn cheese into a dip in a matter of seconds.

Baggies (another registered trademark) give us something in which to put away what's left of the burned roast. They also serve to hold little loose things in a convenient package and have even wound up in our court systems when they are found to contain certain green leafy vegetable matter.

Those were just a few of the things I could think of that have changed our lives as consumers. If I'd had more time, and coffee, more probably could have been added to the list.

(In the 20 years since this was written, we can add CDs, DVDs, MP3 players, iPods, the Internet, cell phones, digital television and a whole bunch of things most of us couldn't imagine then.)

CHAPTER 27
A MATTER OF SIZE

I ran across a story the other day that caught my eye. It seems a gentleman had been forced to drop his membership in a health spa because the other patrons were upset by his appearance.

Now, he did weigh 500 pounds and probably wouldn't have been too attractive in a pair of Jane Fonda Workout leotards, but that doesn't strike me as being a good reason to bar him from one of those places that claim to get people in shape. The place was willing t take his money, after all.

It was particularly aggravating to me that the spa took the action even though the man's doctor had prescribed swimming and whirlpool exercises for a health problem that had forced his weight up. He said the first day he used the spa's facilities he felt better than he had in a couple of months. The next day, the "beautiful" people had their way and kicked the poor fellow out.

Fortunately, the gentleman is suing the spa, which definitely is a blow for those of us who don't have size 2½ waists. I hope he wins because it's time people realized this isn't a 32-scrawny world.

Ever since I was in grade school, I've been somewhat rotund, although I've never approached the abovementioned gentleman's size. I have gone through slim times only to find myself back where I started after a few months. Of late, I've been giving some heavy thought to this matter and have reached the conclusion that it's time we of some heft started throwing our weight around.

Certainly not everyone who carries a spare tire around their waist is attractive, but the same can be said of skinny folks. For example, have you looked at some of these health spa and diet fanatics? Some of these folks are so skinny they look positively unhealthy. They almost could pass as zombie extras in *Night of the Living Dead*.

I'm getting tired of this fitness craze in which so many people seem determined to get themselves back to their birth weight and rake in all the money they can carry. I think Jane Fonda should stick with making movies or political statements instead of cashing in on the exercise fad. I think Victoria Principal should work on improving her acting skills instead of other people's physiques. I won't say anything about Bubba Smith's exercise efforts because I make it a point not to badmouth someone capable of pounding me into the ground with his little finger.

I'm tired of clothing manufacturers making adult clothes that rightly belong in the children's section. Hey, we XL folks like to dress well, too, and most fashionable attire seems made for people who ceased growing in the first grade. I think it's time they started making clothes that fit instead of trying to make people fit the clothes.

It's time for us of girth to band together and say, "We're not going to take it any more!" We're just like everyone else, only there's more of us. Every minority in this country from African-Americans to lisping Lithuanians are organized to make sure no one does anything to insult them. We need to take steps to prevent such offensive action such as what happened to the man at the health spa. I'm not sure what we could exactly do, but there are enough of us that we certainly could strike fear into the hearts of skinny people in America.

We need to accept ourselves for what we are, and so do others around us. We may not always like ourselves, but that's true of everyone at one time or another. It's true we may not be able to use a bandana for a belt, and we may not be attractive in shorts. We may not be able to look like movie stars, and we may not be prize athletes.

But we do have the same feelings as slimmer people and the same wants and the same types of dreams.

All you skinny folks out there think about it the next time you see one of us. We're not going to make fun of you or force you to leave because we don't like the way you look. So, don't do it t us, either.

We ain't heavy; we're your brothers and sisters.

CHAPTER 28
SUMMER COLD CAN COME
IN MANY FORMS

There are few things worse than a summer cold. It's one thing to be hacking and coughing with a runny nose in February, but in June, it's almost unbearable.

Somehow I've latched on to a summer cold this week, and it has just sapped my energy. Of course, some folks might say it doesn't take much to sap my energy, which would be a polite way of calling me lazy.

This time of year I'd plead guilty to that accusation, especially now.

I hate colds and anything associated with them, but they're really despicable in the summer. While those in the medical community contend it takes a virus of some type to cause a cold, I've become convinced through the years that summer colds can be attributed to air conditioning.

Think about it. We go from one extreme to the other by leaving air-conditioned homes, buildings and vehicles for the 80- and 90-degree weather outside. Sometimes we do this several times a day, subjecting ourselves to sudden changes in temperature. That can't be good for you.

Lately, while the thermometer has hovered near 90 outside, here at Sixth and Hickory, you could acclimate yourself for a trip to the Antarctic. I don't want to say it has been cold in our newsroom, but there have been either some short fellows getting ready for a formal occasion, or penguins have been wandering among the desks.

How cold has it been?

Polar bears have asked us to turn up the thermostat.

Every time you open the door, the light goes on.

We've had to add defrosters to our computer terminals.

Frank Wallis has been wearing a sweater in hopes of warding off frostbite.

I've considered setting my desk on fire, but I'm sure that would violate clean air standards and set the EPA after me.

Linda Masters brought us frozen treats, and they never thawed.

While I appreciate air conditioning, I like it in moderation. When I'm driving, most of the time I'd rather have the window down than run the air conditioner. If the pollen count is low, and it's not too hot, I prefer having the windows open at home to running the AC.

I like having a cool refuge every so often, but

under the right conditions nothing beats an oscil-
lating fan stirring the air to cool you.

Now, I'm not a total fanatic. I appreciate step-
ping into an air-conditioned cafe on a hot day, or
stopping at a cool store for a soft drink. I really like
the air-conditioned darkness of a movie theater,
where you can relax in comfort during a matinee on
a hot afternoon.

When I was a youngster, we had a big wooden
box fan in our house. You probably could have used
it to power a swamp boat through the Everglades.
We had it for years, and every summer Mom or Dad
would set it in the hall, turn it on high and let it
blow a breeze through the house.

It also was cool to talk into the swirling blades
and listen to how they gave your voice an other-
worldly sound.

Attic fans always were nice, too. Usually cen-
trally located in a house, an attic fan worked best
when it was reversed, pulling air through the house
and expelling it through the attic. Depending on
how big the attic fan was and the speed you set it
on, you could either have a nice, gentle breeze circulating through the house, or you'd have to strap
down loose furnishings and small animals to prevent them from being sucked into a whirling vortex.

When I was growing up, I don't recall having
summer colds, or other people having them, either.
Back then, most folks didn't have air conditioners,
per se. I remember when we got what Dad called a
water cooler, which was an air conditioner that cir-

culated water through it to cool the air and used fans to blow it into a room. It went into my parents' bedroom because Dad worked nights and slept during the day, and Texas summers weren't compatible with day sleeping.

I don't want to go back to not having air conditioning. I just want to use it in moderation. And I want to get rid of this summer cold, so if anyone would like to have it ...

CHAPTER 29
TURN YOUR RADIO ON

I was playing with the radio the other day while stuck in traffic on U.S. 62 East, which is getting to be a regular occurrence. Getting caught in traffic along Kamikaze Trail, that is.

Anyway, it's amazing what you can find on the radio these days. Since I was in Kim's car, I was able to check out the FM stations. My car has only an AM radio, which means I can pick up two stations clearly in this area during daylight hours, four if the wind is blowing in the right direction. I can get more stations at night, especially those with talk shows featuring such topics as should UFOs be allowed to use international airports and the latest trend in unusual activity among residents of California.

As I flicked the dial, I was able to find a wide assortment of things for my listening pleasure. A little country here, some rock there, a bit of elevator music in between and a few talk shows to round out the selections. Actually, I've found you can create your own radio format by turning the dial at the right times. This usually has some interesting, if not downright unusual, results.

Click.

"Do you have tired, iron-poor blood? Does every day seem worse than the day before? Then try (click) Jiffy Radiator Flush for only $1.50 per quart. Yes, it's guaranteed to (click) add more flavor to your next Sunday dinner. And for even better results with your meat loaf, pick up a package of (click) roofing nails and shingles at Bubba's Lumber Yard. Remember Bubba's motto: If Bubba can't take care of you (click) Willard's Funeral Home can."

Of course, when you start switching the dial between the various talk and news shows, the results can get even stranger.

Click.

"We're talking with D. Hoyle Cargill, who believes the media is responsible for (click) every child born between 1960 and 1980. These people now make up nearly half the (click) population of Red Lick, Ontario. You see, Larry, when Canadians move to the U.S., they (click) can destroy a pine forest in a matter of months with their voracious appetites. In Arkansas, we've been combating this infestation by (click) keeping them housed in a hangar at a secret Air Force base. The government has been hiding this fact from the public since 1949, when it recovered a UFO (click) filled with illegal Mexican immigrants near a weight station outside Flagstaff, Arizona. Authorities said (click) they may become this year's answer to the pet rock. Manufactured by a company in Joliet, they may (click) prove to be the biggest headache for the Reagan administration since (click) Julia Child introduced sardine crepes as the latest in gourmet delights."

You also can create some odd song lyrics by turning the dial at just the right moment, although some of today's song lyrics already are odd enough. And if you're especially lucky, you can arrange even more duets for Willie Nelson.

Click.

"To all the girls I've loved before (click) who work a forty-hour week for a living (click) under the boardwalk (click) down in the Florida Keys (click) driftin' down a dusty Dixie road (click) doin' the neutron dance (click) with me and you and a dog named Boo (click) until the twelfth of never (click) with nothin' but the radio on."

Not even Motley Crue could come up with more unusual lyrics.

So, the next time you find yourself homesteading a car-sized section of Kamikaze Trail, give this little game a try. It'll make the time pass quicker and, who knows, you may never listen to radio the same way again.

CHAPTER 30
ELEPHANT TALK

While looking through an out-of-town paper the other day, I ran across a rather lengthy story about elephants. Now, I like elephants almost as much as armadillos, even if Thomas Nast did besmirch their image by affiliating them, without their consent, to a certain political party.

Since I'm interested in elephants, I took the time to read the article. It seems folks who have been studying elephants for years have discovered they can talk to one another in their own fashion.

According to the story, pachyderms carry on conversations at night on an infrasonic level that ranges from just below on the border of being audible to humans. They also found that some audible rumbles researchers believed were part of the digestive process also are a means of communication among elephants. With this knowledge in hand, scientific-type folks hope they can learn more about the largest land mammal in the world.

Naturally, I began wondering what elephants would have to talk about at night, or any other time for that matter. So, we go now to the African veldt somewhere in Kenya where a group of elephants have settled in for the evening.

"You wanna quit hogging those leaves and pass some over this way? Man, you keep eating like that and you're going to have to go on a diet."

"If it doesn't rain soon, we're all going to go on a diet 'cause these trees and grass are gonna dry up and blow away."

"If you two are about finished, we'd like to get tonight's meeting started."

"Okay. C'mon, Henry, let's go over to the water hole."

"Let me finish flossing my trunks first, Fred."

"I'd be careful doing that. I saw a poacher looking at you the other day with a gleam in his eye. He probably thought your tusks would look nice over some clown's mantle."

"All right, let's come to order. This meeting of the Royal Order of Pachyderms is now in session. We'll dispense with the minutes of the last meeting since Brother Sam forgot them."

"I didn't think elephants were supposed to forget."

"We're not, but you know Sam. He'd forget his trunk if it weren't attached to the front of his face."

"First on tonight's agenda is the question of these folks with that recording equipment over under the baobab tree. There have been come complaints that they've been eavesdropping on private conversations and have been taping them. Are there any suggestions on what we should do? Brother Henry."

"Well, I think we should return the favor one morning. Imagine what they'd do if they woke up one morning and found Fred sitting in their land cruiser."

"Wait a minute. I don't even have a driver's license, and I'd probably get a ticket.

"I think Brother Henry may have something. Let's take his suggestion under advisement. Now, about this Nast character. We've been debating what to do about his making Republicans out of us for a hundred years. It's probably time we did something about it. We haven't been given any royalties, and the few offers which have been made were just peanuts."

"Can we sit on his land cruiser?"

"I don't think he has one, Henry. And besides, I don't think he's a live any more. We could always sue for defamation of character."

"That's probably a better option, Brother Fred. We'll contact our legal counsel and see what he thinks. Okay, that's it for tonight's agenda unless someone had something else. Don't forget – next Thursday we'll have a special screening of *Dumbo* over at the eastern water hole. Refreshments will be provided. If there's nothing else, meeting adjourned."

CHAPTER 31
RETURN OF THE BIG NICKEL

I f the Farmers' Almanac gets its way, the penny and dollar bill will be things of the past, and we'll all be toting around $1 coins. Of course, with $1 coins clanking in our pockets we'll all sound like a 1957 Chevy with a valve problem when we walk.

I ran across a news item this week about the Farmers' Almanac wanting to revamp the national currency system. Now, this is the 190-year-old almanac, not to be confused with the 205-year-old Old Farmers Almanac. On the whole, the almanac's proposal seems to make a fair amount of sense, which probably is why the government won't do anything with the idea.

Unless it leads to the establishment of 32 new bureaucratic jobs, the creation of at least 47 10-page forms and enough red tape to wrap Guatemala, the government isn't overly interested in new ideas. ...

The Farmers' Almanac recommends the government just get rid of the penny, half-dollar and dollar bill. A $1 coin would replace the dollar bill, and the $2 bill, which is probably more used at racetracks than grocery stores, would become the most popular piece of currency, according to the publication.

According to the almanac's figures, replacing the dollar bill with a coin would save $120 million a year. While it costs 2.6 cents to print a dollar bill and 3.5 cents to mint a dollar coin, the almanac points out the bill usually lasts about 18 months before getting shredded whereas the coin would last 20 years.

Actually, the coin probably would be around a lot longer. I still get a lot of 1965 quarters in change, and most are in relatively good condition even after (40) years. In fact, I've seen some (40)-year-olds lately who didn't look as good as a quarter the same age.

Dollar coins – or "big nickels," as my college roommate Toby called them – used to be plentiful. Of course, the last time the government tried to introduce a new $1 coin it went over like a nickel-plated balloon. You may recall the Susan B. Anthony dollar, which most people apparently couldn't distinguish from a quarter, and folks just wouldn't bring themselves to use it. Some even refused to take the coins.

I'm not sure if you can still get any of the small dollar coins, although after the came out people were sure anxious to get them off their hands. I've still got five stashed away with the Latin American coins McDonald's gave away. In Brazil, McDonald's probably gave away Susan B. Anthony dollars with Happy Meals.

The Farmers' Almanac thinks the Susan B. Anthony fiasco would be avoided with the new idea since the dollar bill would simply disappear 18 months after the coin's introduction. That means people would have to conduct their commerce with the dollar coins, which would be dubbed the Columbus Dollar, in honor of Christopher Columbus, and $2 bills.

Besides changing the dollar, the Farmers' Almanac thinks pennies should be discontinued altogether. It said most pennies find their ways to piggy banks, jars and dark closet corners rather than going into circulation, so the government's just wasting money by making them each year. Then again, that's what the government's best at doing, so why should anyone expect it to change.

Should the penny be dropped as a coin of the realm, at least we wouldn't have to carry it around in our pockets with the dollar coins, and it'd be one less piece of metal to rattle.

If we wind up carrying these coins around, we'll have to make a few other changes. For example, pockets would have to be reinforced tin order to carry the extra weight. We'll have to get used to the clinking sound many would invariably make when they walked. And if anyone is prone to rattle the change in their pocket, we'll have to put up with that additional noise, too. That could make standing in a checkout line an even more unnerving experience.

However, I suspect even the benevolent Farmers' Almanac may have ulterior motives in trying to change our currency. I think it ultimately hopes to make the $2 bill, which has experienced more rejection than woody Allen and the Susan B. Anthony dollar, the main medium of exchange and eliminate the dollar currency altogether.

Of course, considering the way prices keep climbing, the dollar probably won't buy penny candy in a few years and will go the way of the penny, although at the moment it's difficult to imagine dollar bills gathering dust in Welch's grape jelly jars.

In the meantime, while we're waiting to see what becomes of the Farmers' Almanac proposal, if you want to get a jump on the situation and feel compelled to get rid of those nasty old dollar bills, just give me a call. I think I can dispose of them for you.

(Subsequently, we did get the Sacajawea dollar coin, and soon we'll have presidential dollar coins available. In the meantime, pennies still are being dropped in jars and dollar bills still are being crumpled in pockets.)

CHAPTER 32
TIME PASSAGES

Did you ever feel like you wait forever to get through the checkout line at the grocery store? Or that you'll be ready for your pension before the red light turns green? Well, you're not alone.

Recently, a management company at Pittsburgh decided to determine how we spend our time so we could learn how to make better use of it. I'm always looking for better ways to use my time, so the story about these folks caught my eye.

Armed with stopwatches, the intrepid researchers went into the world and among their findings were:

- People spend five years of their lives waiting in lines. I can go along with that, although it seems a little short. I wonder if they've ever stood in line waiting to get into a bathroom during the Texas-Oklahoma rally in Dallas. Young people have grown old and suffered kidney failure in that situation. I'd bet they didn't wait in line to get on a ride at Six Flags Over Everywhere amusement parks. People start lining up for those before they're even finished, otherwise they'd never get on.

- People sit at traffic lights for six months. Obviously, the researcher handling this came to Mountain Home where the only things that change slower than the traffic signals are the seasons. Of course, it didn't mention if that was at one sitting per light or for a lifetime.

- The average person spends one year looking for misplaced objects. They never tried to find anything on my desk. It would take a search party accompanied by a Sherpa guide a year just to find a place to start looking for misplaced objects there. And even then they wouldn't be assured of success. In fact, after a recent deluge of business I'm still trying to find the desk. I know it's there ... somewhere.

- We spend eight months opening junk mail like the Publishers Clearing House sweepstakes package mailed to Mr. Baxter Bulletin. Some of us don't bother to open it before it's sent to that great landfill in the sky, so I guess we save some time that we can spend at the traffic lights.

- Four years are spent doing housework. And the place still isn't neat enough when company arrives.
- The average individual spends six years eating. And another six years dieting. Eventually, it all evens out, but I suspect a few of the skinnier people I know aren't pulling their share of the load, and that's liable to throw off the researchers' curve, to say nothing of those of us who have to make up the difference.

Supposedly, the object of such studies is to determine how people can better manage their time. None were mentioned in the story about the researchers, however, there are a few ways we could make better use of our time. For example:

- Take your junk mail with you and open it while waiting in line. If it's something you're not interested in, you could pass it along to the person behind you. He may be the winner, not you.
- Eat while you're doing housework. By following this practice, you get the house clean, enjoy your meal and work off those calories all at the same time. Maybe Little Richard Simmons can come up with a $29.95 video and nutritional program based on it.

- Avoid traffic lights, especially in Mountain Home. Plan your trips so your route will take you around any traffic signals. Not only will this save time, but it also will conserve energy since stop-and-go driving consumes more fuel.

These tips may not actually save time, but you'll be so busy you won't notice you're wasting it, either.

CHAPTER 33
WAR OF THE WORLDSKY

"**U**FO Lands At City Park!"
"Three-Eyed Alien Zaps Teenager!"
"Screaming Crowd Flees Alien Attackers!"

Now, we're used to headlines like that. Every time you go to the grocery store there they are, blaring at you from the pages of publications that make yellow journalism blush.

But this week, the stories behind these bizarre headlines didn't come from a supermarket tabloid. No, friends, they were for stories from the official Soviet news agency, Tass, and Sovietskaya Kultura, another government-run newspaper. So you know the stories must be accurate.

Of course, it sounds as if their correspondents have been practicing a little vodka-nost with the staff of the Midnight Globe.

Normally, UFO landings occur in some backwater, out-of-the-way place where the aliens are seen by a couple of good ol' boys on a fishing trip who caught more Budweiser than bass. Afterwards, people quit talking whenever they enter a room and wink slyly whenever they tell their tale.

This time, the close encounter of a weird kind took place in the backwater, out-of-the-way Soviet town of Dostoevskiburg. While the basic accounts were the same, there were some differences, but that's to be expected in a situation like that. People get excited, and some remember details others don't.

Bubba Karamazov recalled what he saw. "Well, comrade, there were three of 'em, about 13 feet tall," said Bubba. "They had kind of big bodies and little pinheads. At first I thought they were part of some basketball team until they vaporized Josef Bob. I'm sure gonna miss him. He owed me 40 rubles."

Another witness was Billy Sol Tolstoy. "This one alien had three eyes. Kind of reminded me of my first ex-wife," recalled Billy Sol. "He was the one what vaporized Josef Bob. Ol' J.B. was hollerin' something at the aliens after they got out of their space ship – I couldn't understand him – and, before we knew what happened, this alien hauled some kind of gun off the easy rider rifle rack in their spaceship and, ZAP, no more Josef Bob."

"Of course, he always was kind of a loudmouth, if you know what I mean," added Billy Sol. "Never could stay out of trouble."

Mandy Sue Stalin, a waitress at the Dew Drop Innsky, said the aliens came inside the roadhouse and ordered the blue plate special to go. "We get all sorts in here, mostly working class folks, and people from here to Moscow know we serve up a mean blue plate special. So, I wasn't surprised to see these aliens," said Mandy Sue. "They didn't have a whole lot to say, but they did tip well."

Jesse Lee Gorbachev, who runs the local service station, said the aliens stopped at his place for a fill up. "I couldn't find the gas cap on their ship, then one of them fellers picked up the hose and started drinking from it," he said. "I guess they didn't get enough gas from the Dew Drop Innsky."

"Anyway," said Jesse Lee, "once they got their gas, one of them got a handful of Goo Goo Clusters, and borscht rounders, too. He gave me some kind of credit card; I think it may have been a Ukraine Express. They won't let you use a Visa."

Red Barisnykov, the proprietor of Red's Used Cars, said the aliens climbed back into their spaceship after stopping at Jesse Lee's service station. "It looked like a '59 Plymouth, only without the tail fins," is how Red described the spaceship.

"They climbed in, I heard 'em pop the clutch and, whoosh, they were gone," he said. "That was the fastest think without wheels I ever saw, although I think Lonnie Lenin's supped-up Yugo could give 'em a run for their rubles."

That was the last time the good folks of Dosto-evskiburg saw the aliens. However, since the first reports appeared, they've been besieged y reporters and camera crews from around the world. And in this era of glasnost and perestroika, we're learning that even behind the Iron Curtain inquiring minds want to know the untold stories behind the headlines.

(And that even the Reds had rednecks.)

CHAPTER 34
IT'S A BIRD, IT'S A PLANE, IT'S MY INSURANCE PREMIUM

If the cost of insurance keeps going up, pretty soon everyone's going to just wind up endorsing their paychecks to insurance companies to avoid the middleman when paying for health coverage.

Every time you turn around, there's something new about rising insurance costs and rising health care costs, usually an increase. Insurance companies blame the health care industry. The health care industry blames the insurance companies. They both go round and round, and all of us are the ones who go down the financial drain.

I'm not sure who first came up with the concept of insurance, but I wouldn't be surprised if they also developed the first casinos. After all, paying for insurance is pretty much like betting. Paying premiums is like betting you're (a) going to get sick, (b) going to have a catastrophic illness or (c) going to die.

Well, (c) is a sure thing, although it's a bet you don't want to collect on it any sooner than necessary. Some folks are impressed with the amount of life insurance they have.

"Look at me, I'm worth a million bucks." Yeah, stretched out in a metallic grey, satin-lined condo in which your mortal remains will spend eternity. The bad thing about life insurance is somebody else collects it and you don't see a cent of it. When you cash in that bet, you really cash in.

As for (b), there are specific insurance policies for assorted catastrophic circumstances. For example, you can get cancer insurance. If you buy cancer insurance then you must think you have pretty good odds of developing cancer. If you're a smoker who works under the sun waist-deep in PCBs while exposed to radioactive isotopes daily, you might want cancer insurance. In this case, you're betting you're going to contract a dreaded disease.

And when it comes to (a), well, almost everybody gets sick one time or another, so this could be a good bet. Of course, you have to remember that the insurance companies are betting that (a) you won't get sick and (b) you won't have a catastrophic illness.

When it comes to (c), they know they'll have to pay up eventually, so their house bet is that you'll be around longer than you think, paying premiums.

And the thing is, you've got to have insurance. You really can't gamble on not having it. There have been some improvements in insurance coverage through the years, I must admit. For example, I once had a policy that would only pay if I were injured while roller-skating in a buffalo herd during a stampede in a tsunami between the hours of 10:01 p.m. and 10:01:30 p.m. on the Fourth of July in an even year.

Now, I don't have anything against folks who sell insurance. They're trying to make a living and are in pretty much the same leaky boat as the rest of us. So don't all you insurance reps start calling me. Please.

On the other hand, it's understandable that insurance costs keep rising faster than George Bush's popularity at a Baxter County Republican tea.

Health care is the biggest factor, and the most expensive. When it costs a week's paycheck for a bottle with seven allergy pills whose side effects include nosebleeds, exploding heads and unexpected gender change, health care costs are getting out of hand.

Used to be folks could pay for medical care with a couple of chickens. Now it costs the equivalent of a KFC franchise.

And why are medical costs rising? Because of rising insurance costs physicians and pharmaceutical companies have to pay because of people suing them over everything from failed acne treatment to that unexpected gender change. That brings lawyers into the chain, and that's a whole other subject.

As their costs go up, it costs insurance companies more to pay for our covered medical expenses. And when it costs insurance companies more, it costs us even more, at least those of us who can still afford it.

There's got to be an end to this vicious cycle somewhere. Politicians say they'll fix the problem, but when's the last time you saw a politician fix anything? The government says it'll fix the problem, but it -- and the politicians -- probably has done more to make it worse. And I don't think private enterprise is going to do much about it as long as there's someone somewhere raking in the bucks.

In the meantime, we keep getting a walletectomy that has a $250 deductible and $40 co-pay.

CHAPTER 35
SOME HEAVY THOUGHTS

Once again, we're being told we're too fat, and our weight doesn't meet some insurance company's recommended standards for our height, build and gender.

Naturally, I read this little item with some interest since there's no doubt my weight doesn't meet insurance company requirements. In fact, one more or less told me that just this year.

This latest assault on those of us who don't buy our clothing in the kiddy department comes from Prevention Magazine. Based on a random survey of 1,250 people – certainly a good base on which to judge more than 210 million people – the magazine decided about two-thirds of Americans are "too fat."

Personally, I like to think that a third of the population may be too thin.

Prevention also concluded that more than a third of Americans, or at least 10 percent of us, are over the weights recommended by Metropolitan Life Insurance for our height, build and sex.

Have you ever wondered how this company developed its height and weight tables? I mean, did somebody go through his or her office measuring everyone and use that to gauge the rest of the world? And, besides, what makes them so sure that if you're a certain height then you also ought to be a certain weight?

I'll admit if someone is 4 feet tall and weighs 300 pounds, they might have a weight problem. But I think somebody who's 6-foot-6 and weighs 150 also may have a weight problem. They also might have a problem in a strong wind.

Actually, if people followed these tables precisely, then Mike Tyson would be considered overweight. Would you like to tell undefeated world boxing champ Mike Tyson he's looking a little on the heavy side? Do you think you could pinch an inch on Iron Mike's waist, or would even want to try?

OK, that may not be the most accurate example, but who decided these charts were all that accurate? According to some of the charts I've seen, my "ideal" weight would be that of a seventh-grader.

I'll admit I could stand to drop a few pounds – something about half those surveyed wouldn't admit – and I occasionally take a stab at it, usually with some success. But I get tired of surveys that basically say if you don't meet somebody else's standards then you're fat.

And such declarations usually are given in tones that indicate that anyone who doesn't meet those nebulous standards are second-class people who probably should be converted into svelte, aerobicized individuals to thinness or else ignored by those who meet standards.

Personally, I think we need ways to decide if people are too thin. For example, if you don't make a shadow on a sunny day, you're probably underweight. Or, if your nose is the only protruding portion of your anatomy, you're probably too thin.

You're probably under weight:

- If you can use the head of a nail as a campstool.
- If Spandex shorts are too loose on you.
- If you have to wear flippers in the shower to prevent being sucked down the drain.
- If you look like a zipper when you stick out your tongue.
- If people can't tell the difference between you and a broom from a distance.
- If you have to step in front of a mirror twice to make a reflection.

That same Prevention survey said about 65 percent of those questioned felt a great deal of stress at least once a week. I wonder if it's dawned on its publishers that for some of those who aren't a perfect, insurance company-approved height and weight are placed under some of that stress by such surveys.

Maybe it's time to let everyone be themselves, whether they're fat, thin or somewhere between. After all, being content and at peace with one's self has more to do with good health than not meeting somebody else's standard of what we're supposed to be.

(This was before Nicole Ritchie and all the other anorexic-chic starlets came along.)

CHAPTER 36
AT HOME
INTO THE NIGHT

I t's amazing what one can find on late-night television.

Kim and I have been discovering the wonders of that netherworld recently, as one might suspect with a new baby in the house. At one time, I stayed up late all the time and caught the shows that can only be found in the wee hours. Then, my habits changed somewhat, only to have to be readjusted again with Eli's arrival.

The advent of cable and satellite networks certainly has expanded the viewing selection for night owls. Not necessarily the quality, but most definitely the quantity.

Naturally, one can find all sorts of movies on late-night TV. I realize I'm getting older when movies I saw in the theater when they were brand new turn up on the late, late show. Of course, that realization is really driven home when you consider some of those movies are in the neighborhood of 20 years old.

Still, one can find the finer black-and-white cinematic fare with stars like Humphrey Bogart, James Cagney and John Wayne. Then there are the lesser-known movies, although I suspect that in another 20 years some of today's hotly advertised movies will fall into that lesser-known category to a new generation.

Some of these lesser-known old movies are the type film critics call classics. That means they were made before the critics were born. They're scratchy, dark and the soundtracks sound like they've been redubbed over a chainsaw commercial. They have casts of people who may have been up-and-coming starts in 1937, only to become has-beens or never-weres in 1938.

Besides movies, there are other programs to be found after most sane people have gone to bed. For about the last 11 months, two or three of the satellite stations have been running a documentary about famine relief with Sally Struthers. This particular program has popped up at least twice a week on about three different channels, usually after the late, late show goes off. Somehow, I don't think anyone awake at that hour is going to be as concerned with famine relief as they would be a program about insomnia.

My other favorites are the ones that show how to get rich in about 2 ½ hours by buying and selling real estate, even if you don't have a red cent to your name. Yes, according to these personal testimonies, anyone can become a millionaire overnight if you attend their seminars. Somehow, I suspect the seminar would begin: "To become a millionaire, first get a million dollars."

The specialty cable channels offer different types of programs in the middle of the night. For example, one airs a program on microwave cooking, a subject that greatly interests most insomniacs. Another offers an aerobics exercise show, just the thing people want to do at 2 a.m.

The Weather Channel, a 24-hour network with nothing by weather news, provides some interesting viewing. You can keep track of all the latest storm fronts in the Pacific and the temperatures for European cities as well. Actually, it's a very educational channel and perfect for when you get tired of movies and real estate sows.

Then there's Regis Philbin. You can find the man who climbed to obscurity as Joey Bishop's answer to Ed McMahon just about any time of day or night on one particular network. In fact, he's on so often I think it may be the Regis Philbin Network.

My favorite late-night channel is the one the cable company has for weather and announcements of local events. It's almost hypnotic. You just sit there, listen to the elevator music version of '60s folk songs and watch the announcements. Before long, you may not be asleep, but you'll certainly be wishing you were. And in all honesty, at times this channel is better than the others.

So, the next time you find you can't sleep, get up, turn on the tube and scan the channels. You'll be surprised at what you'll find, and how quickly you'll want to be back in bed.

(This was when our son Eli still was an infant, infomercials were brand new and before the digital age and the arrival of 500 channels. One thing that hasn't changed is Regis Philbin, who subsequently zoomed to fame and still can be found everywhere on the TV.)

CHAPTER 37
I FOUGHT THE LAWN, AND THE LAWN WON

You can tell by the sniffing, snorting, sneezing and nose-blowing that I've just finished mowing the yard.

This spring, lawn care has become an ongoing battle around our household. No sooner have I gotten the grass cut that it starts raining, again, and the grass starts growing, again.

I'd promised myself that this year would be different; I wouldn't let the yard get ahead of me. I decided I'd keep it cut and maintain it so it wouldn't look like a hay field.

Well, that was before the spring monsoons arrived.

Now it looks as if the yard should be baled, or perhaps livestock should be grazing on it.

I'm just glad it's grass and not bamboo in the yard. With bamboo's growth rate and all the rain we've received, we'd be living in the middle of a bamboo forest. As it is, there have been occasions this spring that I thought we'd have to bushwhack a way to Amelia's swing set.

When it comes to mowing, I've always had a love/hate relationship with it. I really hate to have to do it, and at one time even wondered how much Astroturf it would take to cover the yard. But when I get started, I enjoy the chance to just guide the mower and let my mind wander. It's a good opportunity to mull over ideas, lay the foundation for columns and, mostly, daydream and meditate.

I've talked about this before. It's what I have dubbed Zen lawn mowing.

Anyway, I've had ample opportunity this spring. As I mentioned, it seems once I get the yard cut, it's time to start over again. What really got me was one morning when it was raining, and I looked out the bathroom window.

I would have sworn I could see the grass growing, the blades slowly getting taller like something out of one of those old Disney time-elapsed nature documentaries.

I kept waiting for flowers to spring up in full bloom.

Then I remembered we hadn't planted any yet.

This time it had been more than two weeks since I mowed. It's amazing how much a yard can grow in two weeks. Now, I'm not saying our yard has been shaggy, but I found a '53 Buick hidden in one corner, next to a Mayan pyramid.

Even Steve Irwin wouldn't get off our patio until the grass was cut.

I realize there's a landscaping philosophy -- now there's an interesting concept -- that recommends letting lawns stay natural and allowing native grasses and plants to grow freely. I could get into that way of thinking, but then instead of a yard I've got a pasture. And along with freely growing native grasses and plants come native reptiles and animals that stay in the tall grass.

I don't like being surprised by reptiles as I go to my truck.

So, I have to mow. And mow. And mow. And mow.

You know, a little of those drought conditions could come in handy about now. Not much, just a little, just enough to slow the growth of our yard. Maybe then I'd have a chance to keep up with it so it wouldn't look like a freshly cut hayfield after I mow.

Well, if you'll excuse me, I notice it's grown about a half-inch since I parked the mower, and there's rain in the forecast. Maybe that free-range landscaping idea isn't so bad after all.

CHAPTER 38
SHOPPING THROUGH THE SUPPLEMENTS

Too much seriousness is bad for the soul and body. It makes you depressed – and depressing to others – as well as tying your stomach into knots and giving you a generally low outlook on life.

For the last couple of weeks, I've been much too serious thanks to congressional pay raises, hood-wearing klowns, murder trials and other generally unhumorous situations. So, I've decided it's time to let my hair down and be a little crazy. Fortunately the Sunday paper provided ammunition for just such an occasion.

I like to look through Sunday newspapers for unusual stories, funny incidents, heart-touching features, a little light reading and those travel pieces that make you want to throw your troubles in your old Samsonite and smile, smile, smile. Sometimes one of those will give me an idea, and I'll make a mental note to file for future reference in that somewhat jumbled filing cabinet in my head.

THOMAS GARRETT

Having had a long week, I really looked forward to last Sunday's papers and the possibility of getting lost among all those pages. As I debated between reading yet another analysis of Gov. Billy Bob's lead zeppelin tax package or "Garfield" – the cat won out – Kim said she'd found something in the Sunday supplement I'd like.

It was one of those shop-by-mail inserts you always find in Parade and USA Weekend. You know the kind, the ones through which you can order two dozen personalized pencils, embossed mailing labels and giant color posters from your favorite photograph.

This one did have a few items I knew I probably couldn't do without, and I was disappointed there was no toll-free number, otherwise we'd have more hi-lo TV poles than we'd know what to do with.

Some of the items you find in these inserts are fairly practical or cute, such as the leather credit card case and the grandmother's sweatshirt with a silk-screened family tree "with the names of grandchildren, pets, etc."

But you really have to wonder about some of the items sold on the pages of these micro catalogues. For instance, I wonder how well the surgical steel multi-blade rotary shear nostril hair trimmer sells. This handy little $6.49 device lets you groom your nose and ears without risking infection by plucking or nicking yourself with scissors.

Then there's Vacutex, a manually operated pump for removing unsightly blackheads without squeezing or injuring your skin. Of course, you never know when you might need what Kim dubbed the Zit Sucker, which costs only $4.49. But, the ad cautions, don't be confused by imitators who would sell you a pseudo Vacutex.

There were other equally interesting items, such as the $3.99 buttoner with which you lasso a button to pull it through the buttonhole, and the $9.99 battery-powered self-electrolysis wand. And for $9.99, you can end the agony of itching with a cream of pine tar and oxide of zinc. I wonder if George Brett's heard about this? Actually, he probably could find a couple of uses for it.

But I was especially impressed by the fresh air in a bottle. It allows you to boost your energy level and reduce fatigue with a breath of fresh oxygen. You can get 20 minutes of continuous oxygen from the kit, which includes a facemask, carrying pouch and shoulder strap.

And it only costs $74.95, with the refill cylinder prices at $18.95.

It's amazing. With a credit card and a stamp, you can end embarrassing itching, get rid of unwanted pimples, trim your nose, button your shirt and feel instantly refreshed.

Thank goodness for America's mail order industry. It places life into a whole new perspective, and enables us to take it much les seriously than we do.

(Then along came e-Bay, Internet auctions and millions of online sources for such wonderful gadgets.)

CHAPTER 39
AMELIA, THE MOSQUITO, THE FLY AND THE FLU BUG

It's amazing how literally children sometimes take what they hear.

Lately, our daughter, Amelia, has been somewhat restless at night and we'd be trying to determine why. This comes after quite an extended period of her being able to pretty much sleep through the night.

Oh, there's been the occasional need for a potty trip, although she's started doing it on her own without waking Kim and me, which I thought was pretty good for a 3-year-old. Out of habit, one of us usually will wake up, listen to make sure she doesn't need any help, then go back to sleep after Amelia gets back in her bed.

But in the last few nights Amelia has slipped back into her old ways, calling for Mama or Daddy, sometimes whimpering or grunting without saying anything until one of us goes to see what's the matter. Often she's still asleep and it just takes a little pat on the back to soothe her.

Of course, that may be three or four or more times a night.

We'd been attributing it to the holidays and the disruption they'd wrought on everybody's sleep cycle. Amelia had gotten to bed a little later than usual while Eli was out of school for Christmas break and we've been trying to get her back into her routine. Naturally, Amelia's resisted, insisting she's not tired even though within five minutes of settling in she's fast asleep.

For a while.

She awakened us several times the other night, rousting Kim most of the time, then me. She wouldn't give any clue about what might be wrong, and actually was still asleep. I finally just closed her door and went back to sleep.

Then, this morning, after another restless night, Amelia gave us a bit of insight.

She was up earlier than usual, and so were we. Mama got the shower first, so Amelia and I got a chance to talk. I asked her if something was bothering her, or if she was having any problems during the day.

No, replied Amelia.

Had her tummy been upset?

No, she answered.

Had anyone been bothering her?

Nope, she said.

Then she got a serious look on her face.

"There's a mosquito."

"What?"

"There's a mosquito in my room at night that bothers me."

OK.

It's January, early winter, and Amelia says there's a mosquito disturbing her. Well, it really hasn't seemed like winter this week. Who knows.

"There's a fly in my room."

"A fly?"

"A fly. It bothers me at night."

Amelia can't stand flies. She delights in getting the fly swatter after them. But a fly in January? In the house?

Neither Kim nor Eli nor I had seen either a fly or a mosquito anywhere, but Amelia insisted both were in her room at night, and that's why she couldn't sleep well.

Now we were getting somewhere. I wasn't sure where, but we were getting there. That's when Amelia put the capper on it.

"And a flu bug, too."

A flu bug? And a fly? And a mosquito?

"Yeah."

Amelia explained that she was afraid the flu bug was going to bite her. She didn't want it to bite her.

That's understandable. Kim got hit with it last weekend, and we've had several friends down with the flu lately. It's not a pretty sight.

And it's been all over television about the current flu epidemic with lots of references to the "flu bug." Even medical professionals interviewed on various news shows have talked about the "flu bug" and how it's making people sick and how so many people are getting "bitten" by the "flu bug."

There are commercials with little animated "flu bugs" and spots for different medicines to take "when the flu bug bites."

It's no wonder a 3-year-old would be worried about getting bitten by the flu bug at night. Especially when she says there's a fly and a mosquito in her room, too. They're real insects, so to a child the "flu bug" must be a real bug, too.

I asked Amelia what we could do about the fly and the mosquito and the flu bug in her room. Without hesitation, she had the answer.

A fly swatter. A pink fly swatter. Or maybe a green one.

She said we could put a fly swatter on the rug by her bed and she could use it to swat the bugs. Then she decided we could hang it from her closet door, and she still could swat the flu bug with it. But she wanted her own fly swatter.

So, it appears the way for Amelia to get a restful night's sleep -- as well as Kim and me -- is as simple as putting a fly swatter in her room. We're going to give it a try. After writing this, we'll all go shopping for a pink, or maybe a green, fly swatter for Amelia.

And she can swat that pesky fly, that bothersome mosquito and especially that obnoxious flu bug.

A VIEW FROM THE HILLS

I'll let you know how it works.

(Amelia received several fly swatters from our friends. The fly, the mosquito and the flu bug all left her alone.)

CHAPTER 40
AMONG LAWN PLANTS,
I'M AN AX MURDERER

I was surprised to discover there's a sidewalk going to our front porch. Actually, I was surprised to find we had a front porch. I just thought there was a trail through the jungle leading to our front door.

Taking advantage of last weekend's sunshine and nice weather, Kim and I spent Saturday trimming shrubs and cleaning the flowerbed in front of our house. As you may have surmised, it had been a while since we last trimmed the assorted flora in front of the house.

Evergreen plants had grown into each other. Pampas grass had intermingled with the other plants. And the groundcover had joined with the evergreens to create their own hybrids. Few things are as surprising as grabbing a vine that leads into a branch that becomes a root so embedded in the ground it makes you actually consider blasting.

Now, I wouldn't say our plant life had gotten out of hand. A bit tall, maybe. A bit spread out, sure. But out of hand, never.

As we hacked our way through the miniature rain forest, Kim and I realized we probably should do this more often.

Anyway, Kim decided there should be a limit on which tools I'm allowed to handle just because I tend to push them to their maximum capacity. Sure, the hedge clippers bent, but that was just because I bit off a bigger limb than they could cut.

And, besides, we managed to bend them pretty much back into shape all three times I bent them. Or was it four?

You just can't let a shrub's limb get the better of you, and sometimes you just have to apply a little extra elbow grease to the clippers.

Kim brought me a saw to remove some of the limbs too big for the clippers. I got most of the way through one limb before the saw blade broke. She says I broke the blade. I say the limb broke it, even if I was putting pressure to it.

Then Kim came up with a hatchet. She figured even I couldn't break a hatchet.

Fortunately, she was right. The hatchet remains intact.

Unfortunately, the same can't be said for one of our shrubs.

It took up a good portion of the bed it shared with other plants. It had entwined with others, so that you had to literally unwrap a limb from the neighboring evergreen.

I used the hatchet to finish cutting the limb that had broken the saw. It took two whacks. There was another limb snaking through the shrub next to it. I managed to get it loose and used the hatchet on it. Right next to that one was another that had gone astray, so I trimmed it with the hatchet.

I thought I was doing pretty good. Then Kim told me there was only one limb left on the plant, and I might as well finish cutting the poor thing down. I pointed out that at least we could get to the water faucet now.

This was the same water faucet that only a short time earlier had been enshrouded in overgrowth like some Mayan artifact. There had been a soaker hose attached to the faucet, but it broke when I pulled it out of the mulch where it had been buried. Pretending it was an anorexic anaconda didn't even evoke a smile from Kim.

Finally, we got everything trimmed and hauled away. So we decided to mow the yard. Well, Kim did the mowing on the riding mower. I did the grunt work with the weed trimmer. I try to be thorough when I use the trimmer.

I take a bare earth approach to lawn trimming. I cut every weed and the grass the mower can't touch down to the ground. That way, unless we're soaked by monsoons as we have been this spring, those areas don't grow as fast and don't have to be cut as often.

OK, so the ground beneath Amelia's swing set looks like a mangy dog with the grass trimmed to its roots. But it's not as tall this week as the yard around it. One thing about our yard is it doesn't need fertilizer. It grows fast and tall enough on its own.

That's why I look forward to dry summers, or at least not having rain every day. For that, I could move to the Amazon. Or Seattle. Whichever would be more hospitable.

It's nice to get out and do work like that every now and then. You feel as if you've accomplished something when you finish. Everything looked so much better, too, except for that small stump by the faucet.

So, if you need your shrubs trimmed, I still have my hatchet.

CHAPTER 41

FATHER'S DAY

There's a lot to be said for fathers and father-hood.

A father is everything in the world to a child growing up. He's the best cowboy, the bravest knight, the smartest scientist, the finest fisherman, most expert woodsman and the best yarn spinner to be found. He's a fearless hero's hero who can slay all dragons lurking in the closet at night and chase off the goblins under the bed, even if they're only shadows and dust balls.

A father can do anything that needs to be done, from putting a wheel on a tricycle to putting a worm on a hook to making a skinned knee feel better. And if he runs across something he's not too sure about, those bright eyes looking up in anticipation provide all the encouragement needed to give it a try.

A father knows the answers to all the questions. He can explain why the sky's blue and the grass is green, why leaves change color in the fall, and why birds go south in the winter. Some questions may be harder for him than others, like where do babies

163

come from, and why can't everyone get along, but he'll do his best to respond.

A father is a teacher who can provide instruction in the important things of life, like how to hold a bat and where to put the batteries in a model car. Eventually, he teaches such things like how to shave and what to do about nicks. And he teaches about things even he may not be aware he's teaching, things like honesty, integrity, chivalry, respect and honor.

A father is a lawgiver, setting out the rules and guidelines that must be followed. He must sometimes impose the penalties that result from violations of those rules, but often the punishment hurts him more than the child even though the child might not know it or agree.

A father doesn't have the easiest job in the world, but it certainly is the most rewarding. No amount of pay is greater than a smile on the face of his child.

Fathers have to watch many changes over the years. They see the different stages their children go through. At some point, a child almost always decides he or she knows more than the father. This can last a long time, but then something else happens, usually after the children are grown. They realize that the older they get, the more their fathers know.

Fathers watch sons grow into men and go on to whatever awaits them. They see their daughters become women and individuals in their own right, even though they'll always be their little girls, no matter what.

Fathers eventually become grandfathers, and at that point life becomes even better. Grandfathers know even more than fathers do and can get away with things fathers can't. It's then that grandfathers truly learn if what they did was right, if they had succeeded as fathers.

And it's then that sons truly realize what their fathers went through, all the happiness and heart-breaks, the good times and the gray times, the fun and serious occasions. When sons become fathers, they appreciate their fathers even more.

I know I do.

CHAPTER 42
WELCOME TO THE OZARKS
ODE TO THE HOOVER HOG

"What is that?"

That's a question posed to me generally by someone pointing in the direction of where my waistline should be. And before somebody comes up with a smart aleck remark, it's not what you're thinking.

It's my belt buckle, or, more specifically, what's on it. The "that" in question is an armadillo.

"A what?"

That's usually the follow-up question asked by unknowledgeable Yankees.

Armadillo. Also known as a hard-shelled possum, possum-on-the-half shell, Hoover hog and other equally endearing names. A creature largely indigenous to the southern reaches of the country, particularly that former republic south of the Red River and north of the Rio Grande where some have started giving it a sort of honored position in the animal kingdom.

Not very many armadillos make it even this far north because the climate tends to be a little cool for them, although there have been occasional armadillo sightings around here. Some people think it's a dumb animal, but considering its avoidance of the colder northern portion of the country, the armadillo probably should be considered among the more intelligent of animals.

The armadillo probably is best known for being a roadside attraction because of its unsuccessful encounters with moving vehicles. I know of no reports of an armadillo ever winning in gladiatorial combat with Detroit's finest. However, it is rumored that the critter may stand an almost equal chance against some of those automotive imports from the land of the rising sun. After all, some of those vehicles aren't much bigger than an armadillo.

Now, some people don't like armadillos. They think they're vile, disgusting creatures. Of course, the same can be said for a somewhat sizable part of our population as well. I agree they can be nasty little varmints when they want to – the armadillos – especially whenever they root their way under a house in search of whatever armadillo delicacies might be there. It's sort of like having a kangaroo in armor jumping against your floor.

Despite the somewhat dingy reputation some have thrust upon nature's little tank, I still must admit a certain fondness for the creature. I'm not really sure what it is about the armored animal that strikes my fancy, however.

It may be their persistence in constantly trying to get across highways and, more often than not, becoming pavement patties. But their descendants continue the quest anyway. Of course, this alleged persistence also could be interpreted as rank stupidity on the part of a creature whose brain cavity is about the size of an extra-large hickory nut.

Another reason for their appeal may be that they have been the object of scorn and ridicule for so many years. No matter what strides have been made in man's relationship with other animals, the poor armadillo has been treated as a second-class creature.

But this may be changing. During the last few years, the lowly armadillo has risen to an almost cult status in some places. You can find its image on shirts, caps, beer ads, posters and other mass-market items, including belt buckles. Business establishments use its likeness and name in their names.

Perhaps the armadillo is finally being given the recognition it so richly deserves. And I'm certainly going to do my part to correct the social injustices inflicted upon this creature.

Armadillo lovers of the world unite!

(Since I wrote this, armadillos have become full-fledged residents of northern Arkansas. Unfortunately, armadillos still haven't figured out how to cross the road.)

CHAPTER 43
OZARK MONSOONS

Monsoon season came a little late this year to the Ozarks, which means we've all gotten to enjoy the pleasures of a sauna and steam bath simply by walking out our front doors.

At this writing, fortunately, it has not rained for about 2½ days, but the clouds keep gathering menacingly each day to hover over our heads and keep us guessing. This has occurred since the last time I mowed our yard. On that occasion, a storm blew in out of the northeast – an odd direction from which to receive a storm here – and drenched everything within a matter of minutes after I'd shut down the mower.

One of my personal superstitions is that mowing the yard, like washing a car, is simply asking for a downpour. Since I plan on mowing this weekend, you might want to get your umbrellas.

It wasn't too long ago I kept hearing people say, "We sure could use some more rain." Once started receiving a daily afternoon monsoon, I haven't been able to find those people to ask them if they think we've had enough yet.

Apparently, all the storms we've had lately are the result of one weather front banging against another, and neither one giving way to the other. As soon as one pushes northward, the other pushes southward, and the rain pours downward.

Personally, I think it's because everybody's been mowing their yards and washing their cars, but no meteorologist will buy that theory.

Now I already know some of you are thinking, "When his yard dries up, and his grass turns brown, he'll be wanting it to rain."

Yeah, I probably will, but that still doesn't keep me from wanting a few dry days. Of course, you don't have to mow brown yards, either.

And I can hear others saying, "It won't be long 'til we'll be wishing we had this rain." These are the same folks who kept wanting more rain. I suspect they may be heavily invested in the umbrella and slicker market.

I guess I really don't mind the rain as much as the humidity after a storm. A friend, Don Green, said it's like Southeast Asia, where it rained every afternoon followed by high humidity. I don't think the humidity would be so bad if it didn't equal the temperature. That converts the comfort index into the discomfort index and gives one the idea of what it's like to be a dishrag.

You can beat the heat, but you really can't do anything about the rain or the humidity. Oh, you

can complain about it and make the traditional ob-
servation that, "It's not the heat, it's the humidity"
that makes it so uncomfortable. But, in the long run,
all we can do is sweat and look for a cool place.

The joys of summer have arrived in the Ozarks.

CHAPTER 44
ACCENT ON THE SOUTH

(In 1985, Chicago Tribune columnist Mike Royko penned a column in which he made several derogatory comments about God's country. A couple of years earlier, he'd written about another trip in which he referred to Flippin, Arkansas, which is just down the road from Mountain Home. I thought it was time to point out a few things to Mr. Royko, especially since at the time so many people were leaving Chicago for the Ozarks.)

It was with particular interest that I read Mike Royko's column the other day. Royko's a syndicated columnist who works in Chicago, so most of the folks around here probably are familiar with him.

What attracted me to this column was his subject – why some folks in other parts of the country are trying to talk like Southerners, with a special mention about them sounding like they came from Arkansas. While there was a slight edge to Royko's comments, they weren't as insulting as his account

175

THOMAS GARRETT

of an alleged passage through the Ozarks a couple of years ago, complete with a degrading description of a hamburger allegedly purchased at Flippin. Generally, however, Royko seems to hold Arkansas and Southerners in low esteem.

According to Royko, Yankees, Midwesterners, Yuppies and others who weren't blessed by being born south of the Mason-Dixon Line think sounding Southern gives them character. Considering the flat, listless and monotone sound some of these folks have, it's easy to understand why they'd want some character in their speech patterns. It's the same absence of accent displayed by television broadcasters and many actors. They all sound generic.

Southern accents do have character about them, an almost lyrical sound unlike any other. Nothing is as pleasant to the ear as a true Southern belle whose accent makes her voice as pretty as a silver bell. And when it comes to storytelling, no other accent adds to a tale like a Southern one.

You have to admit, "ya'll" – as in "Ya'll come back, now, y'hear" – has a much more pleasant sound than the harsh, gruff-sounding "youse" – as the in the oft-heard phrase, "Youse guys down here keep trying to rip us off."

I can understand why someone would rather sound like a Southerner after hearing a litany of "dis," "dat," "dese" and "dose," as in, "Dey never charged dese kinds of prices for dose up north."

And it is a compliment to say that someone would rather sound like and Arkansawyer or any other Southerner than a Damon Runyon character. After all, when was the last time you heard anyone who wanted to sound like they came from the South Side, or the Bronx?

The results achieved by those trying to sound Southern are mixed. I've heard a few attempts at sounding Southern, and not all are successful, like, "Do ya'll give discounts for dese and dose?"

Actually, people using Southern accents even when they're from New Jersey isn't that new a trend. Folk singers who have never stepped foot into the South have been trying to sound like they came form Alabama. Listen to some of those television evangelists. Even the ones from California, New York and Pennsylvania sound as if they spent their entire lives in Faulkner Country. I guess a message of fire and brimstone goes over better when it's laced with magnolia.

If you listen closely to someone from the truly Deep South, you can detect traces of our Anglo heritage. Speeded up, a Southern accent sounds similar to a British accent. Slowed down, it sounds almost Australian. Like so many of the phrases and expressions heard in areas such as the Ozarks and the Appalachians, the Southern accent is rooted in Old English, and scholarly types consider that particular branch of the English language an especially nice one. As you can see, while some folks think Southerners sound like uneducated hicks, we're actually preserving our native tongue.

Make a note of that the next time you hear a true Southern accent, Mike Royko. And, as for that last trip you made to Arkansas, why don't ya'll come back? There still re some folks in Flippin who'd like to talk to you about that.

CHAPTER 45
STAND UP, ARKANSAWYERS

I wonder if Arkansas and Texas got together could they jointly celebrate a tricentennial since both are having sesquicentennials this year? Probably not since whoever got together would more than likely start tossing footballs around and calling each other names.

By now, everybody should be aware that the two states are celebrating sesquicentennials, although I suspect more folks know about the one in Texas than do about the one in Arkansas.

Now, I've got a slight problem with this sesquicentennial business since I'm a native son of Texas and have adopted Arkansas as my home, Of course, I think I'm entitled to Arkansas citizenship as a birthright since my father is a native Arkansawyer, and that makes me half-Arkansawyer.

Naturally I'm proud of the states' 150th birthdays, although some folks would prefer I not mention Texas very much since Texas is getting lots of publicity as it is. And I agree there is something grossly unfair in all this.

I mean Texas gets a book by James A. Michener, a PBS television series and a visit from Prince Charles. Arkansas gets Say McIntosh, Monroe Schwarzlose and a visit from Prince, a black-and-tan coon dog.

Texas, for its sesquicentennial celebration, has reopened an "embassy" in London and named many well-known native sons and daughters as ambassadors. Arkansas ships a National Guard unit to Honduras to trade Razorback souvenirs for bananas and Panama hats.

National television shows have been making special broadcasts from Texas, particularly during this week since Thursday marked the 150th anniversary of the fall of the Alamo and the official kickoff of the sesquicentennial celebration. So far, not even Regis Philbin has as much as mentioned Arkansas' sesquicentennial.

It's been said that Texas has a little too much pride while Arkansas has an inferiority complex. Unfortunately, the latter part seems to be true to a degree, and the former does have a grain of truth. After all, I've never known of a Texan who didn't stretch things a little. Of course, I've encountered some Arkansawyers who knew the fine art of spinning whoppers, too.

But I suppose a lot of it has to do with the stereotypes that developed around the residents of the sister states. The stereotypical Texan is the big, brawny, independent cowboy who doesn't take anything off anyone. The stereotypical Arkansawyer, unfortunately, has been the laid-back, barefoot, moonshine-making hillbilly.

The world pictures Texans as John Wayne and Arkansawyers as Snuffy Smith.

I think it's time Arkansawyers – natives and those who have immigrated here – should show pride in their state, and not just by calling the Hogs. After all, a lot of those folks who made their way to the Mexican state of Tejas and, later, the Republic of Texas and eventually the state, had to come through Arkansas.

To an extent, Arkansas played a small role in the Texas Revolution since Sam Houston is supposed to have made some plans for it in Arkansas. While Arkansas never was an independent nation like Texas and doesn't have as well promoted an image, that doesn't mean we can't be just as proud of our heritage.

We've got just as much to brag about – friendly people, good places to live, beautiful country and abundant water, which is something parts of Texas are lacking.

Don't get me wrong – I'd never knock Arkansas because I'm proud to live in this state. It's just time Arkansawyers united to let the world know we're here, and that we've got just as much to offer as any place else in the world, and more than some.

To paraphrase an old chant: "We're Arkansas. Say it loud, say it proud."

(Since 1986, the year of the sesquicentennial, Arkansas has produced a two-term president and

---

become home of one of the most popular presiden-tial libraries, the world's largest retailer, a few multinational corporations and some of the nation's superrich. Little Rock still wishes it was Dallas, but they're working on it.)

CHAPTER 46
A FAREWELL TO THE FERRIES

Well, the day people around here have been awaiting for a couple of decades has arrived

Yes, folks, the second of two Lake Norfork bridges opens today. There's still some work to be done around the bridges, and they won't officially be dedicated for another month, but from now on people will be able to cross the lake in a lot less time than it's ever taken in the last 40 years.

For some, today hasn't arrived one moment too soon. They're they ones who have known the frustration of waiting in the heat and the cold for the ferries, the ones who have had to time trips to and from town to coincide with the ferries' trips across the lake.

While this is a happy occasion for a lot of people around here, it also is a sad moment.

No more will we be able to take a short, leisurely ferry cruise across the lake and be allowed to enjoy a brief respite from driving. No more will we be able to stand on the wooden deck of the barge, feeling a cool breeze from the water. No more will we be able to step up and talk with a fellow traveler as we cross the lake, to chat about the beauty of the view from the ferry with someone we're not likely to meet again.

It was a Sunday, shortly after I arrived here, that I had my first ferry ride. I had decided to take a drive and explore the countryside. My short journey took me to the Highway 101 ferry landing.

At first, I wasn't too sure about this particular mode of transportation since I hadn't been on a ferry before. From my vantage point on the hill, I got a chance to watch the loading operation, and after a hurried calculation, I found I would get to ride at the front of the ferry in the next group.

I still wasn't too sure about this.

One of the crewmembers directed me to where I was to park my little Nova on the right front corner. From behind the wheel, I could see the end of the hood and lots of water. I made a special point to note where the signs said the life jackets were stored. The tug's engines revved, and we were on our way.

Feeling a little better about the situation, I climbed out of my car since I saw others getting out of their vehicles. I walked over to the railing. As the ferry moved farther from shore, the view widened until you could see for miles down the lake and along its shoreline. It was beautiful, the shimmering water, the boats speeding along through the lake, the green hills and blue sky framing it all.

The water parted before the ferry as it cut its way through the lake toward the landing on the opposite shore. Waves spread across the surface of the lake, some breaking like miniature whitecaps as they reached their peaks.

My worries subsided. This was fun.

The ferry approached the Gamaliel landing, and we returned to our vehicles. The ferry slowed. You could hear the tug cutting its engines, and then the ferry came to a halt with a small thud. Car engines started all around me, so I joined them.

The chain across the front of the barge was dropped, and we drove off the ferry and up the hill, pas the line of cars waiting to cross the lake in the opposite direction.

Since then, I, like many others, have had occasion to curse the ferries and the time it took to cross the lake when I was in a hurry. I've also enjoyed many of the ferry trips I've made across Lake Norfork and, sometimes, looked forward to them.

That's all over now, and the ferries soon will be just memories.

To the ferries and their crews – farewell, goodbye and amen.

CHAPTER 47
OF FIREWORKS AND CHIGGERS

(For about 30 years, there's been a Fourth of July fireworks show on Bull Shoals Lake.)

Sunday night, like a few hundred other folks, my wife, my parents and I trekked to the shores of Bull Shoals Lake to watch the sky explode.

We set forth on our journey well before sunset in the hopes of finding a good spot from which to watch the display. As luck would have it, about half of those few hundred other folks had the same idea.

After winding our way deep into the interior of the Bull Shoals city park, Kim spotted a good place to set up, and we parked the car. From there, we hiked to a spot from which we had an excellent view of nature's stage through a gap in the trees along the lakeshore. It was then we discovered we could have parked the car just in front of where we planned to sit.

Mumbling a few choice phrases, I marched back up the hill, climbed in my father's Chrysler and – probably going the wrong way on a one-way road – moved it to our spot.

Others gathered around our little niche in the trees, but many of them not getting such choice seats as we had.

"Hey, did you bring your chainsaw with you? I've got two trees in my way down here."

Finally, the big moment arrived with a bang as the darkening sky came alive in a burst of gold and blue. Brilliant shades of red, green, yellow, purple and white filled the sky, illuminating the sky and the boats below.

All around us, we could hear a variety of comments from children and adults mixed in among the oohs and aahs:

"Got a big 'un comin'."

Boom!

"Mama, can we get one of those? We could set it off in the yard and nobody would know."

Bam!

"You think nobody in town would know we had one of those?

Boom!

"Got a big 'un comin'."

Pfft.

"That 'un's a dud."

Then, with one final burst of noise and color, the show was over. We waited a while for traffic to thin out before starting our trip home. It had taken less than half an hour to get to the lake from Mountain Home. It took that long to get around the end of the point we were on and headed in the right direction to exit the park.

At an intersection, a dejected-looking officer of the law sat on the fender of his car, apparently surrendered to the idea of even trying to direct this herd of cars out of the park.

But we managed to get out, and then get home with memories of this little excursion.

That wasn't all we brought home.

The next morning, my wife discovered that, despite showering the night before, she was the blue-plate special for about half the chiggers that used to live in the park. If there were a chigger-hunting season in Arkansas, she would have been arrested for being over the limit.

Monday was spent trying to find remedies for chiggers. Standard, over-the-counter medications were tried, then came other suggestions. Fried meat grease, ether, Desenex, fingernail polish. There seems to be almost as many ways to combat chiggers as there are chiggers themselves, but no matter what you do, a chigger will almost always have the upper hand.

Kim tried several approaches to dealing with the little critters – some in combination, although she did avoid the meat grease – and finally began to get some relief by Tuesday.

However, I've got a feeling when I get home tonight I'm going to find she has somehow trained a group of starving red bugs and turned them into attack chiggers with a craving for columnists.

CHAPTER 48
IN THE LAND OF FLIPPINITES AND GAMALIANS

I n London, the folks are called Londoners. In New York, they're New Yorkers, at least in polite circles. And in Paris they're Parisians, unless you're anti-French, in which case they're Parisites.

But what do you call someone from Big Flat?

I had a few minutes on my hands this week and started pondering the various names applied to people from certain cities and states. That led me to wonder what people in these parts would be called, and just how appropriate it'd sound.

Take residents of Flippin, for example. Flippinians just doesn't cut it. Nor does Flippiners. However, Flippinites has a nice ring to it. It's biblical sounding. (Yea, they came from the hills, the Canaanites and the Flippinites ...)

Another biblical-sounding name is Gamaliel, which can be a challenge to newcomers who call it Gama-LEEL instead of Ga-MAIL-ya. Gamalians sounds good, again like something from the Bible, like Thessalonians.

Across the Missouri line, you'd find the Theodosians, which sounds like a name from the Good Book.

Cotterites is another appropriate-sounding name, obviously for folks from Cotter.

Now, Yellville and Gassville are more of a challenge. Yellvillians or Gassvillians doesn't quite sound right. It makes the residents sound like bad guys. Gassvillers and Yellvillers aren't bad, nor are those names.

Lakeviewers could serve as both a name and a description of what folks do at Lakeview; they view the lake.

Folks at Henderson could have a regal kind of sound to their name -- Hendersonians, pronounced like Smithsonian. It just rolls off the tongue, Hender-sooo-nians.

Over in Marion County, would people in the Eros community be the Erosians?

Or maybe the Erotics, which certainly might raise an eyebrow or two.

Calico Rock residents would have a cool name, the Calico Rockers. In that musical vein, could people at Viola be Violans?

I really have been perplexed on what people from Bull Shoals would be called. Bull Shoalians? Bull Shoalins? Bull Shoalites? This is a tough one.

Midway residents could be Midwayans, not to be confused with members of the Wayans family of comics and actors.

Down at Buford, they could be Bufordians, or Buforders. Both sound pretty good.

Of course, I can't forget Mountain Home. This is one I've thought about for a while. In fact, it's the one that set off this whole process of pondering names.

Mountain Homians just doesn't sound right. Neither does Mountain Homites.

Then, it came to me.

Mountain Homers.

Yeah, that has a good solid ring to it. Mountain Homers.

"Where are you from?"

"Why, I'm a Mountain Homer."

It would fit well on a bumper sticker, and it'd work on T-shirts, too: "Proud to be a Mountain Homer," or "Another proud Mountain Homer."

This may be something the Chamber of Commerce should think about.

Now, about people from Big Flat, what would you call someone from there?

Like Bull Shoals, Big Flat presents a challenge. Big Flatter? Big Flattian?

Big Flatite? Big Flatso?

Of course, all of us are part of one big family, whether by birth or choice -- we're Arkansans. Or Arkansawyers. Or Arkies. Take your pick.

CHAPTER 49
OBSERVATIONS FROM A COUNTY FAIR

By now, everyone should be recovered from their outings to the Baxter County Fair. All in all, it appeared to be another success, if a fair's success can be judged by the number of cotton candy-covered kids waiting to get on rides. Or by the number of people who register for prizes ranging from free trips to skate boards.

As I was attempting to scrape someone's discarded gum from the sole of my shoe, I formed a few observations about what I'd seen at the fair. First of all, gum and gum chewing should be banned at any public event unless it's part of a bubble-blowing contest.

Based on the number of abandoned wads I had to sidestep – and the two I didn't see – it would appear many folks have no qualms about just tossing their used gum wherever they please. Trashcans, or even wrapping it in a piece of paper, seem to be concepts that totally elude them.

People who throw gum on the ground, like those

who stick it under seats and tabletops, should be rolled in used Juicy Fruit and dumped on the court-house square as an example to others.

A fair is an excellent place for people watching. Practically everyone goes to the county fair, even folks who don't get to town more than once or twice a year. Some of the people I saw at this year's fair looked as though they hadn't been out of the woods since LBJ was in the White House.

The contrasted nicely with the folks dressed in the latest fashionable attire. Denim obviously still is the main fabric of choice based on the assortment of denim clothing in assorted conditions folks were wearing. While I've got a couple of pair of faded jeans – one naturally faded, the other with a store-bought fade – I still haven't fathomed why ripped clothing is considered fashionable.

One youth I saw looked as though he'd just fin-ished the wildcat wrestling competition. It appeared a single, long thread held his tattered sweat shirt to-gether while his jeans looked as though he'd been wading in a piranha pool. He probably paid more for his ripped shirt and jeans than they were worth simply because they had somebody else's name was on them.

I think charitable organizations could double their takes by offering worn-out clothes as the latest in high fashion and charging high fashion prices.

Maybe I'm starting to show my age a little, but I'm not sure I'll ever understand the urge to pay big bucks for clothes that make you look like a refugee from a Bush Hog accident. And I still haven't figured out why folks aren't embarrassed to wander around some place like the fair dressed like that, especially those of the female persuasion who have to pay particular attention to where the rips and tears are so they don't reveal more than they intend to show the world.

Down along the midway, things hadn't changed this year as barkers barked and shillers shilled, trying to convince everyone they could win fabulous prizes worth far more than the dollar-a-try for their games. In all my years of fair going, I've never won, or seen anyone win, a prize that couldn't have been purchased at a discount freight sales store for about a tenth of what it cost to play the game and win the stuffed critter.

Of course, everyone loves a challenge, and few things are as challenging as trying to beat a carnival game. There are some games that flip the cynical switch in the back of your head. You know the type, such as the one where you knock a stack of cans over with a ball; yet not even Nolan Ryan could fell some of those stacks.

However, some of the carneys were good with the little ones, giving them all the chances in the world to win cute little prizes. I appreciate that because to a little boy or girl plucking three ducks from a water tray or snagging a brown paper bag filled with unknown treasures can be a highlight of his or her fair trip they'll remember for the next year, no matter what they win.

After three relatively long trips to this year's fair, I'd had enough fun and excitement, and I'd registered for more drawings than I can recall and nibbled on more cotton candy than I should have, although I didn't get my annual candy apple this time. Of course, before we realize it it'll be fair time again soon enough.

In the meantime, maybe I can get all the Wrigley's Spearmint off the sole of my shoe.

CHAPTER 50
A SPECIAL THANKSGIVING

(On Nov. 18, 1985, a tornado cut across the Ozarks, tearing through Marion and Baxter counties and Mountain Home. Several homes were destroyed and damaged, as was the Pinkston Middle School gym and other structures.)

W e have much to be thankful for this Thanksgiving, even though at first glance it might not appear that way.

In only a matter of minutes Monday, the lives of many in Mountain Home and Baxter County literally were turned topsy-turvy at the hands of nature. Many won't be able to gather their families around the dining table this Thanksgiving because they don't have a dining table. Some won't even be able to spend this day of thanks in the comfort of their homes because they no longer have homes.

Yet we all still have our lives. Through some turn of fate or miracle or what have you, no one died as the tornado churned its way across our county, ripping whatever got in its way to shreds.

199

There weren't even any serious injuries here. As one gentleman said to me, it's something that will make you stop and think there is a higher power looking over us. For that, we can be truly thankful.

The tornado had barely passed before neighbors began helping neighbors. In the pitch-black darkness of Monday night, with rain soaking everything and everyone, people who did not suffer from the storm – and some who did – gave their assistance to others. Homes were opened to friends and relatives. Even strangers have offered to let folks whose homes were damaged or destroyed move in with them for a while.

No matter what one thinks of human nature, and despite those who make one wonder if there is indeed any goodness left in the heart of mankind, when something like this happens cynicism falls away as hands are extended to the unfortunate. That can renew you faith in people.

Yet while people are doing what they can to help, there are some who are trying to take advantage of disaster. Some are out there preying on the elderly and those who can't help themselves. Some are thinking only of their wallets when they ask if they can help, looking to earn a profit from the misfortune of others. Every disaster, it seems, attracts its share of jackals and vultures in human form. People should be wary, and those unscrupulous "helpers" should be sent packing back to whatever rocks they crawled out from under.

So much has been written and said about the terrible events of Monday that people may be getting tired of hearing and reading about it. Yet there are some things left to be said and thanks to be given.

As quickly as possible, firemen, policemen, their auxiliaries, city and county workers and volunteers responded to the emergency. Many were doing their jobs, but some took those extra steps, which made their efforts, in the words of an oft-used phrase, above and beyond the call of duty. Many whose own homes had been struck by the twister went to work trying to evaluate the situation and get it under control. Some who weren't even on duty, and were even on vacation, dropped what they were doing and jumped into action.

There were those who work for various utilities who stepped in to do the dangerous work few of us would want to do. In the rain, in the dark, they began looking for downed power lines and getting those lines – many still hot and dangerous – back up so we all wouldn't have to spend the entire time in the dark. They put in long, hard hours, and no one can say they didn't earn their pay. While we may all gripe about our utility bills, none of us would begrudge these people who came through and put the lights back on.

The Red Cross, the Office of Emergency services and other agencies responded as quickly as they could to help. They're still working today to see that no one goes cold for lack of a place to stay or hungry for lack of food.

Yes, we do have much to give thanks for this Thanksgiving. When those of us who were untouched by nature's fury sit down for that annual dinner next week, let's remember those who were and not forget that the day means more than turkey and football.

CHAPTER 51
ROLLIN' ON THE RIVER

L iving in the heart of trout country, some of us occasionally overlook what we have right here in our front yard.

It had been quite a while since I'd been on a float trip on the White River. When you don't have a johnboat, float trips can become somewhat infrequent, and I don't think you could get much fishing in floating on an inner tube down the river. Besides, you could get in real trouble if you hooked the tube.

So, when my friend Less the turkey farmer called the other day, I was quick to accept his invitation to take a float trip and see how many trout would ignore us. I think one of the last float trips I'd taken had been with Les, and that was more years ago than I should admit. Most of my fishing in the interim has been pretty well confined to bank fishing, which still is fun, just as not much fun as floating the river.

Sunday morning began early enough. Kim nudged me awake, telling me it was after 6, and I was supposed to meet Les by 7. After getting up and getting around in the dark, and looking at the clock on the TV cable box, it dawned on me Kim hadn't fallen back the night before, and it was only 5:30 in the morning.

Oh, well, at least I was wide awake by the time I met Les and we headed for the river.

We fished out of the Norfork Trout Dock with Dwayne Jones as our guide. Hitting the river not long after 7:30, and with Dwayne at he controls of the motor, we were on our way downstream in low water. The weather could not have been improved on during the whole day as we motored down river.

It's amazing how clear the water is on the White. You can see everything through the crystal water, from silvery trout and camo-like suckers – and even an occasional smallmouth – to the glimmering shadows of brown and red and tan rocks lining the river's bottom. Near Porterfield Estates stands a deep green moss ebb and flow in the river's currents.

Trees bearing fall colors lined the banks and framed the pale bluffs towering above the river. Along one stretch of the river amidst trees and houses the new Arkansas state flower was in bloom, catching television signals being beamed from space.

And in the middle of this, there we were, sitting in a 20½-foot johnboat, scaring trout. Actually, we did rather well for ourselves. While some folks fish only for the big ones, we just wanted to catch fish.

And catch fish we did.

Dwayne set us up in areas where the trout were plentiful and ready to bite. Rare were the times when we'd cast a line that we didn't at least get a nibble. We also spent a fair amount of time stunning nightcrawlers as we slapped them against the water. At the end of the trip, Dwayne knocked the corn still on his hook off by hitting the end of his rod in the water. Les and I had been doing that occasionally throughout the day.

Usually, despite our sometimes-crude casts, there'd be small trout on the ends of our lines, although Les did bring in a couple of other catches. Once, Les reeled in one of the largest suckers I've seen.

Despite its coloring, a sucker isn't the prettiest of fish. It's better looking than most catfish, and probably on the same par as carp, but it's never going to win any beauty contests.

A little later, Les hauled in what he dubbed the "White River monster." Instead of a trout, he caught trout bait – a rather large crawdad. It was a sizeable crustacean, which Les contended thought it was an Alaskan king crab. I suspect by now it's grown even more in the telling.

Midday meant a shore lunch of freshly caught trout and potatoes cooked in a sizzling iron skillet, home-baked bread, slaw and beans. There, on a gravel bar under a bright blue canopy of sky, Dwayne cooked up a meal unrivaled by any of the chefs at the fanciest of restaurants. Of course, those places couldn't even come close to the ambiance of a White River cookout.

205

Back in the boat and motoring upstream, we teased a few more trout and surprised some suckers as we headed for the dock. It was late afternoon with the sun beginning to edge past the hilltops when we scraped over a couple of shoals and pulled in at Norfork.

Pleasantly tired, Les and I realized that sometimes you can go too long between such jaunts. A trip down the river is one of the best ways to clear the cobwebs from one's head and become reacquainted with what we tend to take for granted. Hopefully, the time between this trip and the next won't be measured in years.

CHAPTER 52
REMEMBER WHEN?
WHEN CARS WERE CARS, AND GAS WAS CHEAP

Who would have thought $1.22 per gallon gasoline would sound good?

That's what the price was in Mountain Home 25 years ago in the midst of a gas war, according to an upcoming look at news of yesterday. Ah, the good old days. That's when one fast-food place offered a burger, fries and a drink for $1.84.

You can't even get a gallon of gas for that now let alone a meal that could give you gas.

With the price of gas heading toward the stratosphere, it makes you long for the time when gas was cheap. I remember pumping gasoline for 29 cents a gallon when I worked part-time at Joe Minnick's service station in DeKalb, Texas. And that was for premium.

For that 29 cents, along with gasoline you got your windshield washed, your oil checked and free air for your tires while you sat in the comfort of your vehicle. Now, for the premium price of about

THOMAS GARRETT

$2.35 a gallon and more, you get out of your car, pump your own gas, wash your own windshield, check your own oil and air your own tires. What's wrong with this picture?

When I was in high school (and yes, we had cars then), my buddies and I could chip in a quarter to 50 cents each, fill up the tank on one of our cars Friday night and cruise around town all weekend and still have fuel left Monday morning. I paid more the other day to gas up my lawn mower than we paid to fill up a friend's 1957 Chevy (which hadn't reached the classic car stage then).

Now, if four or five friends pool a quarter each they might get a half-gallon of gas and they should be able to drive home, if it's not too far.

Those were the days when cars were cars and gas was cheap. Those were the days when cars were still made of steel, six- and eight-cylinder engines were the norm and aimlessly driving from one end of town to the other was a relatively cheap way to pass the time.

Now, cars are made of plastic, six-cylinders are considered high-energy engines and driving from the garage to the end of the driveway is a relatively expensive trip.

Other than to stop driving, I can't think of anything folks can do about the price of gas. OPEC has the United States over a barrel, and oil companies have the rest of us over a barrel. And the cost of the barrel keeps getting higher. Sure, there was a report the cost dropped a little, but you can bet it'll be back up there soon.

It has been suggested that everybody in America not drive for one day and not buy gasoline for one day. That would show the oil companies what for, costing a day's sales and cutting into their profits. While that sounds good on Internet chats and in e-mails, it would only put small stations out of business, hurt the little guy and disrupt everything in the country.

Besides, you can't get everybody in America to agree on whether Pepsi or Coke is better, so how are you going to get them to not drive or buy gas for a whole day?

There's always the possibility of converting diesel vehicles to run on vegetable oil. I was reading that the guy who developed diesel originally had a means of using vegetable oil as a fuel. That could be promising; just pour some Crisco in your tank, and you're ready to roll.

Willie Nelson is using vegetable oil to fuel his tour bus. Now when you get behind Willie's bus you still get the munchies, but have an overwhelming urge for fries.

We could go back to using horses and buggies, but then you've got that little environmental problem horses leave behind, and we already have politicians putting out more than enough of that stuff.

We could start using electric cars, but where could we find extension cords that long, and how could we keep drivers from getting them tangled?

THOMAS GARRETT

We are going to have to do something because we can't just keep paying higher and higher gas prices, just as we can't keep driving bigger and bigger vehicles that use more gas. I saw an SUV the other day that could double as a school bus. I've seen SUVs that are bigger than some of the apartments I've had. I saw one at a station the other day getting gassed up, and for what it cost to fill its tank my high school friends and I could have cruised for three years.

I just hope that in another 25 years somebody doesn't look back and say, "Who would have thought $2.50 per gallon of gasoline would sound good?"

CHAPTER 53
A LITTLE PULP CAN TAKE YOU A LONG WAY

In these hectic times, there's nothing quite as re-laxing as a nice trip up a jungle river, dodging spears and avoiding headhunters.

Or perhaps just taking a nice, quiet trip island hopping across the South Pacific, dodging pirates and looking for lost treasures.

Maybe even a trip to the Far East, trying to un-ravel some of its inscrutable mysteries.

And do it all without ever leaving home, except in your imagination.

Lately my interest in pulp fiction has been un-dergoing a revival of sorts. I've always liked rock 'em, sock 'em, two-fisted action/adventure tales that take you to exotic locales with rugged heroes, feisty heroines and dastardly villains. You know, the kind of stuff moms usually thought were a waste of time. (Although my Mom did occasionally read some rather pulpy stuff herself.)

Of course, many of today's best-selling genres -- mysteries, Westerns, science fiction, fantasy, horror -- can trace their roots to those pages of cheap paper wrapped in lurid covers.

My reading tastes cover a wide range, enough so to be considered quite eclectic. Actually, I'll read almost anything. In times of desperation I've been known to read can labels and food boxes.

Occasionally I'll latch onto a particular topic or style for months, reading everything that catches my interest in that genre. Sometimes my interests overlap, and it's not unusual for me to have two or three books going at a time.

Recently, I've been reading *The Lord of the Rings* that Eli bought me; *Band of Brothers*, Stephen Ambrose's account of a World War II paratrooper company; some Louis L'Amour adventure stories, prompted by promos for a TV movie based on one of them, and the basis for my pulp fiction revival; and I've picked up a Harry Potter book, although I haven't started it yet. (I read what I can when I get the time, and usually have a different book at different locations.)

But it's pulp fiction that's always been a mainstay for me. I remember when I was in high school I became somewhat enamored with Richard S. Prather's Shell Scott mysteries and Donald Pendleton's Mack Bolan series, both extremely pulpy.

In college, I got hooked on stories by Robert E. Howard, who created Conan the Barbarian. I also became a fan of The Shadow, Doc Savage and other assorted pulp characters who were going through a brief revival.

Then I discovered Travis McGee and John D. McDonald.

These days, there still is plenty of pulp fiction around; it's just printed on better paper and costs more. Clive Cussler, one of my favorite writers, probably would have been one of the top pulp writers 60 years ago. His Dirk Pitt novels have all pulp mainstays -- a handsome hero with loyal sidekicks, damsels in distress, fast-paced action, large-than-life villains and more plot twists than a jungle river.

There's just something about these stories that hold a magic allure to me. Perhaps it's just a way to vicariously journey around the world and have adventure after adventure. Of course, that's the point of almost any good writing, to put the reader in the heart of the action.

Few do it as well as pulp writers and their modern successors. With terse dialogue, vivid descriptions, marvelous metaphors and wild, yet plausible, plots, they weave magical tales that take us away from dreary everyday life. Who could resist the promise of untold treasures, or the seductive wiles of a femme fatale, or the challenge of overcoming overwhelming odds?

So, the next time you feel like a little excitement or want to get away from the workaday world, find something with a little pulp to it.

You'll enjoy the trip.

CHAPTER 54
POPSICLE MEMORIES

Another American institution is headed down the road to nostalgia. I ran across a story this week that announced the two-stick Popsicle soon won't be available in grocery stores.

It seems the Popsicle makers have given in to complaints from mothers that the two-stick Popsicle was too inconvenient and messy, so starting this spring only one-stick versions – to be sold in boxes of 12 – will be put in supermarket freezers. The two-sticker still will be available at convenience stores, amusement parks and from sidewalk push-carts, but I suspect that won't last much longer.

For more than 50 years, the two-stick Popsicle has been as much a part of spring and summer as baseball and swimming. The original purpose of the two-sticker was so two friends cold split one Pop-sicle, thus providing a lesson in sharing as well as refreshment.

But mothers – who never seemed to appreciate the importance of such things – felt the two-sticker was too big for their children to handle and was too messy since it often started to melt before it was finished, And moms tend to have their way eventually. While the story said mothers were the primary Popsicle purchasers, everyone knows kids are the primary Popsicle consumers. I've never seen a kid yet who couldn't handle a Popsicle, and usually the messier it was, the better it tasted.

Oh, for the days when all the cares of the world could fade away with one lick of a cherry Popsicle. Grape and orange Popsicles also had the power to solve difficulties and relieve the heat. The Popsicle's ice cream cousins – the chocolate Fudgesicle and orange-flavored Dreamsicle – also had those miraculous powers.

And the fun didn't end when the Popsicle was gone, either. When you finished eating the cool confection, you had two sticks to play with. With a little imagination, one could make a reasonable facsimile of an airplane with nothing more than two Popsicle sticks and the sticky residue left on them. The more industrious of my childhood associates would clean their sticks and save them for more elaborate projects. Many a vacation Bible school class has turned out Popsicle picture frames.

Before he passed away, Kim's grandfather created Popsicle stick lamps, one of which we have. It works better than the factory-made lamps we have.

And it was the desire for a cherry Popsicle that sent me on my first covert mission when I was about 5. We lived two blocks from a small mom-and-pop grocery store, and one summer day I developed a craving for a Popsicle. Company was over that Sunday afternoon, so it would not have been proper etiquette for Mom or Dad to take me to the store.

So, already having the necessary 10 cents in my pocket and not wanting to bother my parents, I struck out on my own in search of the fabled Popsicle.

Being Sunday afternoon, there weren't too many folks stirring, and I didn't have to worry about traffic along Browning Street. Carefully following a course along the correct side of the street, I made my way to the store, which sat beside a state highway. There, with all the deliberateness of H.L. Hunt picking an oil lease, I chose just the right cherry Popsicle.

My decision was based on the heft of the icy treat, its bright red color and the number of ice crystals that had formed on its wrapper. Having picked what had to be the tastiest of the Popsicles from the ice cream freezer, I handed the lady working behind the counter my 10 cents.

I unwrapped my treasured treat as I'd been taught and properly disposed of the wrapper in a trashcan before starting back home. Oh, it was so sweet and cold and refreshing as I walked back up Browning Street licking my Popsicle. When I got back to the house, I discovered I hadn't been missed. It wasn't until I told my parents about my little sojourn that they realized I'd been gone. Fortunately, I received only a stern lecture about wandering off on my own and was advised to seek permission before making any future road trips.

I hadn't thought of that little adventure until I saw the Popsicle story this week. And since it had been a while since I'd had a Popsicle, I stopped off at E-Z Mart to buy one. A cherry Popsicle. It cost a little more than 10 cents, but it still was just as refreshing as Popsicles ever were.

And it had two sticks, just as a Popsicle should.

CHAPTER 55
THE CLASS OF '72

L ike the lyrics in the Statler Brothers' song, we all thought we'd change the world with our great works and deeds.

We were the Class of '72, the pride of DeKalb High School. Let me make this perfectly clear up front – it's DeKalb, Texas, not even remotely close to that other DeKalb up north.

When we got our diplomas, everyone had plans – and dreams. We were proud, full of fire and ready to make the world do double back flips if we wanted.

Well, Friday night, a few members of the class of '72 got together for an 11–year reunion to see how we're doing. We missed the 10th year, but, then again, we sometimes had a habit of not always following tradition. For many of us, this was the first time we had seen each other in a decade plus one year, even though some had not left that sleepy Northeast Texas town where we were raised.

DeKalb is the kind of town that could have been used for *The Last Picture Show*. The last picture show in DeKalb was shown many years ago, and the old theater became a furniture warehouse. I've gone back to my hometown every time I had a chance, but I rarely got to see any of my classmates. Time has a way of separating people even if space doesn't.

Nothing really changes much in DeKalb. Just last week a man claimed a rancher there tried to lynch him for rustling. The pace of life there is about the same as it was 11 years ago, the same as it was 11 years before that, and probably the same as it will be 11 years from now.

With that in mind, I wondered how we in the class of '72 had fared. How had we changed? How had we spent those 11 years after we marched out of the high school gym in our caps and gowns on a warm spring night?

A couple of us had sprouted beards. Fortunately, none of our female classmates had grown them. Hair was thinning on some, and waists were thickening on others. A couple appeared unchanged.

Several of those in attendance work at the defense plant where many of our fathers worked. At least two classmates became salesmen -- one selling restaurant equipment, the other handling the southwest region for a tire manufacturer. I learned the quarterback who married the cheerleader is in the military, as is another classmate.

One of the pep squad members sells ladies ready-to-wear clothes in a shop in DeKalb. Another married a man in the oil business and now describes herself as "a lady of leisure and tennis bum." Yet another works at a hospital in Texarkana.

Two of us wound up in the newspaper business. Two became doctors. One of the cheerleaders married a doctor. Two graduates from our class are providing free labor for the state.

We all had a laugh when one of the coordinators of our reunion said another classmate wanted to be there and put on a show, something he'd always been good at in class. Then we learned he's a professional dancer in Dallas. He didn't make it to the reunion, however.

On the whole, we turned out to be pretty average, normal folks trying to make a living, not exactly the earthshakers some of us expected to be.

Some have achieved at least part of their plans. Some have had to change their plans, and some – like the dancer – apparently got a whole new set.

We still haven't changed the world, but you never can tell.

The class of '72 still has its dreams.

(This was our first class reunion, in 1983. There have been a couple more since then. One classmate went on to be a TV producer for professional golf. The ones in the military already have retired, and I saw one of the doctors one night on a Discovery Channel show. Me, I'm still a newspaperman.)

CHAPTER 56
THE LAST GREAT SAFARI

Deer season starts Saturday. Which means if you're going into the woods you'd better wear lots of bright orange clothing unless you want to become a trophy over someone's mantelpiece.

Fortunately, around here there haven't been that many hunting accidents in the last few years, and, hopefully, there won't be any this year.

It's been a long time since I've been hunting. In fact, I was still in college the last time I went into the wilds in search of game. Several college buddies and I ventured out in search of the elusive quail on that last great safari.

We were an odd-looking assortment of sportsmen. One wore an old pith helmet, another had on a straw cowboy hat that was long past its lifespan, there were a couple of military surplus caps and baseball caps covering heads. We had enough artillery to start a small firefight. In fact, we looked like a ragtag group of South American guerillas.

THOMAS GARRETT

We spread out in a line and marched across a wide, open field, which was waist-high in grass in sots. For one of our number it almost was chest high. Slowly, with careful, calculated steps, we stumbled across the field, waiting for the fat little birds to take wing before us. We were ready.

Suddenly, a bird flew up a few yards ahead of us. It wasn't a quail, but that didn't matter to some in our little group. Three or four opened fire, scattering shot like anti-aircraft bursts in the air. When the smoke cleared, the bird was gone.

Not dead, just gone. It flew away, untouched, unharmed and unscathed.

After some good-natured kidding and a short debriefing session on what went wrong, we continued our march. By the time we crossed the field, the only thing that had been flushed was the flying escape artist and an assortment of insects.

We sat around for a while, trying to decide what to do next. As the afternoon wore on and the boredom level increased, we became more desperate to find something to shoot at so we wouldn't go back empty handed. Then, someone declared it was pith helmet season and tossed the headgear into the air. Shotgun blasts shattered the quiet of the Saturday afternoon as the hapless helmet rose into the air, then descended to the earth. Like the bird, the helmet escaped uninjured. Unlike the bird, it got a second chance and was tossed into the air.

Again, the group opened fire. This time, someone hit the pith helmet on its descent, knocking it back up into the air for a second.

This went on for several minutes, and the unfortunate helmet was hit a couple more times. Finally, growing weary of the target practice, one of our number just shot the helmet as it lay on the ground to put it out of its misery. This prompted others to do the same, and in a matter of seconds all that remained was a limp object that bore a strong resemblance to Swiss cheese.

Looking back on it now, I realize it wasn't exactly the most sophisticated outing, but it was fun for the moment, and it was good training. I mean, after all, you never know when someone might declare pith helmet season again.

CHAPTER 57
APPRECIATING THE FINER
POINTS OF CALENDARS

I remember this was the time of year when Palmore Drugs always handed out its new calendar, the one with ads for Black Draught on it.

If you didn't like that one, you could always go across the street to the Rexall Pharmacy and pick up its calendar with ads for various over-the-counter medications.

That's where people used to get their calendars, the local drug store. Banks always were good about providing calendars, too, and so were the local grocery stores. But in our household, it was the drug store calendar that we used to chart out our schedules for the coming year.

My cousin Roy Lee ran an auto body shop for a few years and his tool distributor always left him a calendar. As a youngster, I wondered about the appeal of a smiling, scantily clad model holding a Snap-On Tools belt sander.

As I grew older, I came to better appreciate the finer qualities of power tools and the marketing of them. I didn't even mind going to the parts store for my Dad because they got tool calendars, too.

You can still get free calendars from businesses. They know its something people use almost every day, and whenever anyone looks at it there's the business' name looking back. With tool calendars, the business name became more of a subliminal element.

Now there are lots more calendars out there, but you have to pay for them. When I was growing up, it seemed unheard of to pay for a calendar. But times have changed.

Fans don't mind having to buy calendars featuring their favorite actors and actresses, scenes from a favorite TV show and movies or photos of their favorite music stars. Whether you like Ozzy Osbourne or Alan Jackson, there's a calendar out there for you.

There are artists' calendars that have reprints of paintings by artists such as Thomas Kincaid. Besides having something to keep track of important dates, at the end of the year you have a set of prints suitable for framing. They may not appreciate in value, but it is an inexpensive way of collecting art.

(I understand one Civil War artist caught on to this and stopped producing calendars with his work a few years ago.)

There's the "Worst Case Scenario" desk calendar. It has lots of helpful hints that could come in handy if, oh, a rhino charged your desk. Or you had to save a customer from a crocodile in the office. I guess you could adapt those tips for dealing with irate customers.

One calendar I've wondered about is the "Left Behind" desk calendar. Since the "Left Behind" series is, basically, about the last days of the world, I suppose this calendar could come in handy, although it seems a bit incongruous to me. Unless, of course, all the pages after a certain date are blank.

If the world's on its last legs, wouldn't a watch be more practical than a calendar?

And then there are the cheesecake and beefcake calendars. There are swimsuit calendars, although they have more calendar than swimsuit. There are calendars that feature the girls of Texas and California and the hunks of the New York City Fire Department.

You can even special order calendars for charity. The latest craze is fund-raising calendars by garden clubs, quiltmakers, fishing clubs and so forth that feature members in their birthday suits. Usually there's a strategically placed gardening instrument or quilt patch, and usually many of the members remember when FDR was in the White House. And when the raciest thing about calendars was ads for Carter's Little Liver Pills.

Before you know it, somebody will have a calendar featuring grannies holding Snap-On Tools belt sanders.

CHAPTER 58
WHAT HAS HAPPENED TO
BASIC SNEAKERS?

Have you noticed it's almost impossible to find a pair of just plain sneakers?

You go to the store these days and they've got running shoes, jogging shoes, walking shoes, tennis shoes, work shoes, hiking shoes, deck shoes, shoes for almost any and all endeavors, including some for which shoes aren't necessarily required.

But the basic sneaker seems to have gotten trampled in the rush to develop specialty shoes.

Whatever happened to Keds, the sneakers that made you run faster and jump higher? The ones I had didn't improve my speed or my jumping abilities – I've always run like an injured yak, and my knees have never been too excited about jumping – but they sure were comfortable.

It used to be that every kid around wore sneakers, generally black ones with white trim. Black sneakers concealed dirt better and, therefore, could be worn much longer than white ones. White sneakers with black trim were usually reserved for more formal occasions.

Black sneakers with white trim also looked neat when worn with blue jeans that had cuffs rolled up on the legs. Of course, then your jeans were dark blue when you bought them and faded with wear. By the time they looked like some of the new ones you can buy in the stores now – at quadrupled price – they were ready to be converted into cutoffs or patches.

Oh, I suppose there are some shoes on the market that technically would qualify as sneakers by their design, but I'll be darned if I'm going to wear eye-blinding blue, phosphorescent pink or seasick green sneakers. Or the ones that look as if they've already been worn by exceedingly sloppy painters.

Nowadays, instead of sneakers we've got to choose from among assorted athletic footgear, some of which come with the reminder they aren't meant for everyday wear and potentially could cause foot problems. You could wear sneakers until they fell apart – and we usually did – with no worry other than getting water through the two little air holes on the sides.

And instead of being made of cloth or canvas with rubber soles, today's athletic shoes include plastic and vinyl in their construction. Plastic and vinyl make my feet perspire profusely and give off a not-so-aromatic aroma. Today's athletic shoes just aren't as comfortable as yesterday's sneakers.

I found a pair of sneakers about a year ago –

white with dark blue trim – for $7, and they've served me well. They're not quite suitable for all occasions now thanks to too many and well-ground grass stains along with considerable wear and tear. What can you expect for seven bucks these days? But they're still comfortable and great t slip on in the evening or on Saturday morning.

A few weeks ago, I found a pair of canvas shoes. They aren't exactly sneakers, but they're suitable. I've been wearing them to work and on semi-formal occasions. They have the potential of becoming a well-liked pair of almost sneakers.

Still, it would be nice to find a pair of Keds.

(Keds have made resurgence. And along with my usual boots and substitute sneakers, I've discovered the joy of Crocs, those rubber shoes with the holes that are so comfortable.)

CHAPTER 59
A LETTER FROM HOME

I couldn't believe it. There it was, in black and white, an Associated Press story about my hometown, DeKalb, Texas – not to be confused with that other DeKalb some folks around here would be more familiar with.

Actually, the story was about the main tourist attraction in town, the grave of Dan Blocker, known to anyone who ever watched Sunday night television as Hoss Cartwright. Now, that might seem a somewhat macabre tourist attraction, but think about it a minute. The pyramids attract thousands of tourists, and they're just huge tombs. And how many people visit JFK's grave in Arlington National Cemetery each year?

So, why can't the final resting place of the man known as Hoss be an attraction? The only other claims to fame DeKalb has are what is supposed to be the biggest bois d'arc tree in the state of Texas and the legend that Davy Crockett named the place while on his way to the Alamo.

THOMAS GARRETT

DeKalb was Dan Blocker's birthplace, and, weighing in at 14 pounds, he was the largest baby born in Bowie County. He maintained his huge stature throughout his 42 years. When he was in the service, he had to have custom-made size 14EEE combat boots. His stature helped bring him fame as the gentle giant of TV's Cartwright clan. When he died in 1974, he was returned to his hometown for burial in a funeral, which, for a moment, brought national attention to DeKalb.

His mother, known to most folks around town as Miss Mary, lived in DeKalb until last year (1984) when she moved away to be with her famous son's family. Miss Mary was a sweet lady whom everyone in town liked. Whenever I went home, if there was news about her, my folks were quick to tell me.

Reading the story took me back to that small East Texas town just south of the Red River. There were a few familiar names in it, like Roy Blankenship, owner of Roy's Chicken Shack, and Orval Miller, who owns Miller's Grocery. (After his retirement, my Dad helped out for a while at Miller's Grocery.) Robby Bates, the local funeral director and an old friend, was even quoted in the AP feature.

I haven't gotten back to DeKalb in a while, so the story brought back some memories. It was almost like a letter from home. Anyone who has traveled U.S. 82 west through that part of Texas has been through DeKalb, whether they wanted to or not. It's just west of Malta and east of Avery.

DeKalb isn't a big town, probably about the size of Yellville for those wanting something familiar to compare it with.

It's the home of the DeKalb High School Bears and the award-winning DeKalb High School Band, of which yours truly was a member many years ago. Now I've got some cousins who are in the band and are helping carry on the winning tradition.

DeKalb has changed since I lived there last. Joe Minnick's service station where I once worked is closed, and Mister Joe is long since gone. Most of the stores downtown have changed or are gone altogether. The old movie theatre closed while I was in college, and for the last few years has served as a furniture warehouse. There's a grocery store and pharmacy at the site where the old one-room city jail was located. A new carwash is just across the street.

On my last visit there, however, I noticed some things were still the same. The East End Garage is still on the west end of town. I never could understand that. The high school kids still cruise the main drag between the railroad crossing across from Miller's Grocery on the east end of town and the overpass west of town, as we did when I was one of them. Still, it seems more has changed than has remained the same.

I get The DeKalb News, which along with almost every other paper in the county is published by a guy I went to high school with. It has the local news and happenings, but seeing an AP story with a DeKalb dateline was different. It was as if my hometown had finally been recognized.

Thanks, AP, for the letter from home.

(Since I wrote this in 1985, DeKalb has seen many changes. Fire destroyed the high school I'd attended, a tornado knocked down much of downtown and it became associated with another celebrity – it's where Rick Nelson died when his plane crashed.)

CHAPTER 60
THE LAST SODA FOUNTAIN

It's been said a man can be judged by the number of friends he has. I'm not sure who said that originally, but using the comment as a jumping off place, I'd say Howard Baker likely would receive a favorable judgment.

Several of his friends were on hand this week to help him celebrate his birthday at the place where he cold be found for more than 30 years, Baker City Drug on the square. Gathering in the vinyl-cushioned booths and sitting on the chrome and vinyl stools at the soda fountain, they came to wish him well on the start of another year of life which began when Woodrow Wilson still occupied the White House.

There's no telling how many prescriptions Howard has filled there just off the northwest corner of the square. Or how many questions he's answered about what this prescription will do for those symptoms and how often it should be taken. One might be hard-pressed to determine how many times over the years he personally delivered a prescription to a customer unable to get out because of illness or bad weather or whatever reason there might have been.

Equally as important, at least to some of us, is that it probably would be impossible to calculate how many cups of coffee Howard and his wife Dorothy have poured for the morning and afternoon coffee crowds. Coffee at Baker's is practically a daily ritual for many here. In the last three decades, wars have been started and finished, inflation and deficits have been curbed, and innumerable social ills have been resolved over coffee in Baker's booths.

Almost every morning, the Baker Drug Irregulars come and go through the plate glass door. They discuss the news of the day, then turn the conversation to the really important topics – the Cardinals, baseball in particular and sports in general.

Occasionally, there have been other subjects for consideration, such as the sinking of the Invictus II, which was skippered by Baker Drug Irregular Bud Carney. References still are made about that event nearly two years later.

It's like the old gatherings at the soda fountain after school used to be, only there's a greater variety of ages. Actually, Howard Baker has the last honest-to-goodness soda fountain in town. You can see where, over the years, knees have rubbed the sheen and color from the vinyl covering on the bar while customers sat and turned on fountain stools. Coca-Cola glasses line the shelves in front of the mirror behind the fountain, along with paper cups, heavy porcelain coffee mugs and those crystal-like sundae and soda glasses.

Accumulations of aircraft memorabilia, airplane magazines and golfing magazines attest to Howard and Dorothy's interests through the years, as do the cameras on one wall. When they're not in the store, you're likely to find them on the links pursuing par.

There aren't many places like Baker City Drug any more, nor druggists like Howard Baker. The new, fast-service, medications-only pharmacies just don't have the same atmosphere you can find at a place like Baker's, a place where friends and memories can be found.

So, for all the years of service, the filled prescriptions, the coffee and just for having a haven for a brief respites from the day's activities, thanks, Howard. And happy birthday.

CHAPTER 61
FRIDAY NIGHT HEROES

Tonight will mark the official kick-off of high school football season in Mountain Home. While I've never really gone overboard about sports in general, I am interested in a few, and high school football is one of them.

Around here, there's a fair amount of interest in high school competition, but not as much as in some places. I suppose since so many of the people living here came from somewhere else and are retired, meaning they generally don't have anyone in school here, it's hard for them to get worked up about it.

But in many places, high school football stops short of being a local religion. When I was going to school in Texas, the games of autumn probably rivaled the wars between the city-states of ancient Greece. Every Friday night, any town that had even a hundred-yard long cow pasture and some bleachers fielded the cream of its local youth crop against other towns.

Now, these folks took their high school football seriously. They pumped themselves up all week for the game, big or small, with all the fervor of the most fanatical Muslim. Posters were put up in store windows and throughout the schools. Ribbons bearing slogans such as "Swat the Hornets" and "Skin the Leopards" were sold by pep squad members for a dime, although inflation raised the price to a quarter by the time I got out of high school.

A pep rally topped off the preparations, most often on Friday afternoon if it was a home game, Friday morning for road trips. The Friday night heroes sat on the stage of the gym while cheerleaders led cheers and the band played the fight song. The coach would have a few words of encouragement, and the principal would give a short speech. The quarterback, joined by the team captains, would describe what they intended to do, although not as graphically on stage as they did among their peers.

By game time, the stands were filled with proud parents, cheering cousins and roaring relatives. People who didn't even have anyone in school, or whose children were only in elementary school, turned out. At DeKalb, the band boosters ran the concession stands, and they were ready to sell popcorn, hot dogs and Frito pies, along with Cokes, Dr Pepper, Seven-Up and big orange drinks.

And so it began, adrenalin filled teenagers smashing into one another for the honor of their schools, towns and themselves. In the heat of September and the sometimes bone-chilling rains of November, these young gladiators fought to be the best around. They played with the ferocity of their mascots' names, pushing continually for the glory of the goal line. Nothing was as sweet as the taste of victory, or as bitter as the feeling left by defeat at the hands of a long-time rival.

But in the case of defeat, there was always next year, when 17-year-old veterans and 15-year-old rookies took the field.

Saturday morning would find the usual crowd at the café, sipping coffee, eating biscuits and gravy and analyzing the previous night's action. They had more opinions than Carter has little pills and offered their advice to all within earshot of them.

Everyone knew everything about what went right and what went wrong. They knew what the coach should do, who should play and which players should stay on the bench. It's easier to coach from the coffee shop than the sideline.

What they had to say didn't matter, however. By Monday, the community was gearing up for the next game with new posters and new ribbons. Autumn was an exciting time in small-town Texas thanks to high school football. In towns where nothing much ever happened, people enjoyed the excitement and thrills given to them by their Friday night heroes.

CHAPTER 62

GOOD EATS
SOME LIKE IT HOT: CONFES-
SIONS OF A FIRE EATER

I suppose you could call it an addiction because once you start, you're hooked. It's sort of like drinking, or narcotics, or *Star Wars*.

My habit started innocently enough. First it was black pepper, just plain, common black pepper. Everyone uses it. Then it was Hunts' spicy catsup, something that's not even on the market any more as far as I know. From there I moved to the next level, spicy mustard. I'm not sure anyone else in high school who brought their lunch used such an exotic condiment on their pressed ham and cheese sandwiches.

Then came Tabasco. For generations, this has been the hot sauce of choice. Made with fiery peppers grown on Avery Island and aged in oak, this Louisiana treat is a worldwide favorite. It can be found in almost every household and in restaurants from the greasiest greasy spoon to hautiest haute cuisine establishment. Even the military issues tiny bottles of Tabasco in the MREs it supplies our gallant fighting men and women.

Whether shaken on scrambled eggs or splashed into gumbo, Tabasco enhances the quality of any dining experience, and provides just the right kick. I once made some homemade Tabasco sauce using peppers Dad grew in the garden. The pan I used could not be used for anything else afterwards unless you were making a hot dish. But this was just the beginning, the gateway to the hard stuff.

Next were jalapenos. Now these truly were hot manna from heaven. Freshly picked and crunchy, they spread their scorching flavor throughout your mouth was you munch them. Their cool-looking, bright green skin belies the fire within. For me, fresh jalapenos tingle my tongue and scorch the walls of my mouth, growing in intensity as I keep eating them. Stuffing shredded cheese into them doesn't degrade their power, but enhances it for me. When you slide the stuffed fresh jalapenos under a broiler for a couple of minutes, letting the cheese melt, it only doubles the illicit pleasure you get setting your mouth on fire.

Pickled jalapenos are what make nachos nachos. Without the peppers, they're just chips and cheese, snack food for wimps.

It didn't stop with Tabasco and jalapenos. No, there were more torrid foods out there just waiting for someone else to fall victim to their enchanting spells. The more I found, the more I wanted, the more I craved peppers and dishes that left me with charred taste buds.

Dips and salsas that lay the faint-hearted low became an early favorite. At a Corpus Christi eatery, I once ladled up a heaping helping of a green salsa onto a chip and took it in one bite. It was pure, condensed fire. The waitress left a pitcher of water on the table. Stephanie, who works on the other side of the room here at Sixth and Hickory, once brought another green salsa to the office for a potluck lunch. In small doses it could bring tears to your eyes. In large quantities it could bring EMTs to your side. My, it was good.

Bamboo Gardens introduced me to the delights of kim chee, which must be Korean for "flaming cabbage." Definitely an acquired taste, kim chee is a fermented dish of cabbage and hot peppers -- a sort of blazing sauerkraut -- that can clear your sinuses and give you a whole new outlook on life.

Of course, I can't leave out hot wings. Kim makes the best wings around. After we got married she, too, became enamored with spicy food and hot wings is her spiciest dish. With a hot sauce and some butter Kim can make chicken wings that, as Tennessee Ernie Ford once said, make you slap your grandma on the run.

She's experimented with different sauces, from Crystal Hot Sauce to one with habanero peppers. Each has been unique, yet linked by heat. As you eat the wings, you find yourself being consumed by the desire for more. No matter how hot, no matter how much your mouth may burn, you keep dipping back into the pan, unable to resist.

Kim may have reached the pinnacle of her hot wing quest with a batch of wings she made this week. She used a sauce that came in a bottle with a white label and a picture of a man in a sombrero on it. It proved to be liquid fire. These, without a doubt, were the hottest hot wings Kim has ever made.

With these wings, a fire-eater could achieve a flaming nirvana, the ultimate plane of pleasure for those who like it hot. Even as my tongue smoldered, I couldn't stop. I continued committing arson against my mouth. As blistering as the wings were, I kept going back for more even though I knew I'd pay for my overindulgence later. It didn't matter. Even as my face turned red, perspiration popped from my forehead, my eyes teared, I continued until even I reached the point I couldn't take the heat.

So, yes, I guess you could call it an addiction, this taste for fiery food. But what a wonderful addiction it is.

And I haven't even tried Thai food.

Yet.

CHAPTER 63
IF YOU REALLY WANT TO EAT, FRY, FRY AGAIN

OK, now let me get this straight.

French fries are supposed to be carcinogenic under the right conditions, grilled red meat can become a carcinogen and anything that can't fit in the palm of your hand is too big a portion to eat.

So, does this mean we're back to the Yogi Bear diet -- nuts and berries? I hope not, although I do like nuts and berries, especially on ice cream.

Every so often, the so-called "experts" announce they've discovered this food or that food is bad for us. Usually it's something that tastes good, like French fries and grilled steaks bigger than a deck of cards. A few years ago it was Chinese food, pizza and popcorn, three staples of my nutrition pyramid.

What they say is good for us usually tastes like sawdust soaked in Elmer's glue. Nutritionists suggest we should eat things such as tofu. We can have all the veggies we want because they're good for us, at least if they're either uncooked or undercooked, but man does not live by brussel sprouts alone.

Of course, I have to admit we as a society have taken to somewhat unusual cuisine. For example, who else would have thought of deep-fried cheese as an appetizer? Or pizza with more cheese in the crust alone than Wisconsin can produce in a month? The general consensus here at Sixth and Hickory is that you should just inject cholesterol directly into your arteries.

Then there's one of my favorites, fried corn on the cob. Sure, it's a bit extreme but it's also mighty tasty.

I guess having grown up down south in Texas helped set the course of my dining habits. Although it has been a while since I was down Texas way, as I recall there were two main food groups -- fried and salad bar. Grilling was just a way of frying without the pan.

Anything that could fit in a skillet could be fried. Meat, potatoes, eggs, vegetables, even bread. And if it could be fried, then it also could be deep-fried, usually with a generous coating of batter.

Fried food is part of our heritage. Until Paul Prudhomme burned a catfish filet one time and called it blackened catfish, the main way it was prepared was frying. No one ate catfish unless it was fried, along with hushpuppies that also were fried.

Dip hot dogs in the hushpuppy batter and throw them in the fryer and, presto, corn dogs.

Fried chicken, chicken-fried steak, chicken-fried chicken, fried fish, fried shrimp, fried pork chops and so forth. The only thing that comes between us and our main course is a crispy coating and, occasionally, white cream gravy,

Now, I'm sure the "experts" and others might be shocked by such food and would encourage us to eat more healthy stuff. But tell me, have you ever tried chicken-fried tofu?

Thought for the Week: "If you are what you eat, then I'm fast, cheap and easy."

CHAPTER 64
ANOTHER FADING ROADSIDE ATTRACTION

Fast food places have taken the adventure out of traveling.

I reached that conclusion on the road back from Texas last week. More and more people are chowing down at the fast-food places that are springing up like mushrooms everywhere.

Don't get me wrong. I've been known to frequent fast food places and, generally, I've enjoyed some of their fare.

It's just that a piece of Americana is fading away along the highways of our country. It's getting harder to find a meal that comes on a real plate with real knives and forks and glasses. Nowadays, food is served in Styrofoam cartons – which sometimes are tastier than their contents – with plastic utensils and drinks in paper cups.

I remember riding along with my folks on vacation and seeing al the roadside cafes, their brightly colored neon signs flashing and cardboard signs in windows announcing the day's special.

Sometimes we'd stop at one of these eateries, a practice which increased over the years. There were times when we ate bologna, cheese and crackers purchased at some mom-and-pop store instead of stopping at a café.

A couple of places stand out when I recall travels with my family. One in particular was a hot dog stand called Dan's in a south Arkansas town whose name I can't remember right off hand. Dan's dished up the best hot dogs I'd ever sunk my young teeth into.

They were meaty hot dogs served on fresh buns with pretty near whatever you wanted on them. With one of Dan's hot dogs, some French fries and an icy Coca-Cola in you, you could resume a journey with your hunger completely satisfied.

These days, however, travelers just don't stop at places like Dan's as often as they used to do, which has meant the demise of many of them. Unfortunately, I'm as guilty as anyone else.

I guess people appreciate knowing exactly what they're getting when they stop to eat now, which can make sense considering the price of everything nowadays. Everyone knows the food at a national burger place in Arkansas will taste the same as that at one in Maine or Idaho. The food's safe and filling, but it doesn't offer the culinary adventure eating at those small roadside cafes could.

In fact, after eating in these spots for a while, the food not only tastes alike, the people working in them even begin to look alike.

A VIEW FROM THE HILLS

Every so often, I still like to try those small places along the highway that aren't affiliated with anything except the local chamber of commerce. Sometimes you can find a roadside café whose food would make you slap your grandma on the run, whose blue plate special would shame alleged fancy restaurants.

You also can find places where today's special is yesterday's reject and tomorrow's swill. And the old saw about food being good wherever truckers eat doesn't always hold true. A lot of truckers are satisfied with anything that fills them up, and some of the worst food I've had was eaten at truck stops. I remember one truck stop that a special so bad you could have lubricated a fleet of trucks with it.

But that's part of the adventure – finding which places have good food, and which ones should be avoided at all costs, unless you have your own personal stomach pump.

Think about it the next time you're on the road. Do you really want another burger with the secret special sauce, or would you rather take a chance on finding the best meal you've had since your mama fed you?

CHAPTER 65
BUFFET BUFFOONS

B uffets and salad bars are interesting places to observe the human parade. Watching some people crowd around them is sort of like watching a National Geographic documentary about animal watering holes.

I like going to places that offer buffets and salad bars with broad expanses of taste-tempting treats from which you can pick and choose. In many restaurants, the salad bar has become a virtual institution, and other places offer buffets, either daily or on weekends or both. The nice thing about them is you get to see what you're about to dine on without having to wait and wonder what it's going to look like when the meal is brought to your table.

Now, while most folks show the proper etiquette when going through a buffet line, there unfortunately is another breed that takes advantage of the offerings – the buffet buffoons.

You've seen them. They're the ones who act like they've been kept caged somewhere for months without being fed and escaped only moments before descending upon the restaurant.

They rush the warming tables within a split-second after the newest item is brought out, trampling everything and everyone in their path like a herd of thirst-crazed longhorns that just smelled water. Woe to the innocent bystander who was getting small second helping of mashed potatoes at the time. Insurance companies do not sell policies that cover injury or death at the bands of buffet buffoons.

Within a matter of seconds, before anyone else even has a chance to budge in their seats, the buffet table has been picked clean. The buffet buffoon stragglers growl and snarl at each other as they fight to get the last green pea left in the bowl. Like hyenas, they circle the table, glaring at one another and making tentative thrusts with their forks at the sole pea until finally the stronger of them spears it and rushes to his table in triumph with his trophy.

There are other types of buffet buffoons. For example, there's the hoarder. This particular individual is deceiving as he or she makes one trip around the buffet table or salad bar to fill a plate. Then, when the hoarder thinks no one is watching, he or she returns and fills up again, often getting the last of some items.

Back at the table, still trying to make sure no one sees, the hoarder begins wrapping the food in napkins and stuffing it into coat pockets or a purse or whatever is handy. Like a squirrel preparing for winter, the hoarder now has a second meal – for the price of one – to be eaten later at his or her lair.

Then there is the one who tried to blend in with everyone else, but just can't get the hang of it. This one breaks into line to acquire one item, then decides he needs to get a few other goodies while there. Generally, this will be his second or third trip to the buffet.

Another buffet buffoon is the type who breaks into line and, when he's ready to leave, bumps into you or knocks something from your hand or even nearly knocks you down without ever saying, "Excuse Me" or "Kiss my grits."

As I said, most folks show the proper etiquette in buffet lines, and the restaurants do what they can to make sure everyone gets what they want and enough of what they want. They want to keep their customers happy, but even they can't help the behavior of the buffet buffoons.

I don't know about you, but one think I've had enough of is the buffet buffoons. The next time you see someone exhibiting such rude behavior, if you point out to them that they're being buffet buffoons, we might someday make them and endangered – if not extinct – species.

CHAPTER 66
CHILI WEATHER

The first true chilly weather of autumn has arrived, heralding the arrival of chili weather.

Yes, when those first signs of frost appear on the grass in the mornings, when you have to wear a jacket for the better part of the day, when you begin turning up the heat and building fires in the fireplace, it's chili weather.

When your breath forms little puffs of steam in the morning, when the leaves begin changing from green to red, when the high for the day doesn't come close to 70, it's chili weather.

This time of year, there's nothing better than a big bowl of steaming chili. Nothing else knocks off the chill like chili. And, depending on how spicy it is, chili has been known to keep you heated up for a couple of days.

There are as many ways to prepare chili as there are chili peppers, and almost everyone who has a fondness for this dish has their own recipe. The unfortunate thing, however, is that it seems not too many people can properly prepare this meaty manna from heaven.

The problem is beans.

True chili, as true chili aficionados know, doesn't have – or need – such an ingredient. A wise chili cook once said if you know beans about chili, you know there are no beans in chili. Of course, this point has been debated since the first person dropped a red bean into a chili pot.

It's been debated in my home ever since I got married. Kim, raised on non-Texas style chili, prefers hers with beans. So, rather than risk starting a continuing gourmet battle, I compromised and found a fairly decent recipe calling for chili with beans. And, much as I abhor this desecration of chili, I have to admit that at least this particular version is tasty.

But I still prefer mine beanless.

From the chili I've sampled in this neck of the woods, I've discovered much of the local chili is made with beans. Not all of it, but a large percentage of it does contain beans.

In fact, some of it would be laughed at South of the Red River. It isn't really chili, but a bean soup with a little meat and chili powder in it. It's what I call New England-style chili, a variety developed by the same kind of people who soak steak with catsup and think cornbread is something only the Waltons eat.

That kind of chili wouldn't stick to the floor let alone your ribs.

Someone else – a Yankee, no doubt – developed a strain of chili made with beans and spaghetti. Now this definitely is a different view of chili. (Since my mother-in-law makes a variety of this chili, I'd best be careful on this point, at least if I intend to keep getting an occasional meal from her.)

I suppose it's just southwestern chauvinism, but I just can't get used to these unusual varieties of chili. For my own tastes, give me a bowl filled with hunks of meat seasoned to perfection with chili powder – or, even better, chili peppers – garlic, black pepper, maybe a touch of tomato or tomato sauce and a little onion, along with a few other secret ingredients I toss into my chili pot. Now that's chili.

To borrow a phrase from a chili commercial – friends, how long has it been since you've had a big, thick steaming bowl of chili? Well, hoss, that's too long.

(These were some of the tastier words I've had to eat through the years. I still like beanless chili, but I've found a couple of recipes that use beans and produce a pretty fair pot of chili. My mother-in-law still uses spaghetti in her chili.)

CHAPTER 67
GOOD TO THE LAST DROP

A man without his morning coffee is not a pretty sight.

After giving the little one his bottle Sunday morning, I headed for the kitchen to prepare my morning formula. But when I pulled off the canister's lid, I discovered to my horror that there wasn't enough coffee to make half a sip. Hurriedly, I checked the kitchen cabinets for any – yeech – instant coffee, which is a poor substitute at best. Alas, there was none to be found.

By now, a mild panic was setting in, and I was getting desperate. I was willing to try anything. Let me tell you, Dr Pepper is no substitute for morning coffee.

Finally, after getting my wits back, and on Kim's suggestion, I took the thermos and went to get some freshly brewed coffee at one of the local eating establishments for immediate relief. That would do until more coffee could be purchased for home use.

I first began drinking coffee at an early age. Everyone in my family is a coffee drinker. You can't go into any of my relatives' homes without finding a pot ready. Should there not be any ready, it takes only a moment to get a fresh pot brewing.

In many societies around the world, but particularly in America, it seems coffee is the ultimate beverage for all occasions. Deals can be made over Folgers. Personal plans and problems can be discussed and worked out between sips of Maxwell House. A brief respite from a hectic day can be found in a cup of Maryland Club.

Coffee, unlike other beverages, complements any situation, and rather than giving you a hangover like the proverbial three-martini lunch, coffee can help you recover from the effects of said lunch. It should be noted, however, that coffee, as amazing as it is, can't cure intoxication, as some believe. All it does is keep an intoxicated individual awake.

In the newspaper business, coffee ranks right up there with ink and all the other necessary requirements to get a paper out. One of my journalism teachers told me that, after the basics, the first rule of the newspaper business is to learn where the coffee pots are on your beat. The second most important rule is to find the locations of the bathrooms on your beat.

Unfortunately, there is an effort afoot these days to discourage the consumption of coffee, or, more specifically, caffeine. Scientists have concluded that if you give a white rat 50 gallons of coffee an hour it'll stay awake and irritated, so humans probably shouldn't ingest anything containing caffeine.

Decaffeinated coffee is the pits. It's worse than instant coffee, all of which tastes the same no matter what Robert Stack says. Drinking coffee without caffeine, to quote Bear Bryant, is like kissing our sister. Why would anyone want to drink coffee without caffeine since that's what makes coffee coffee?

The same goes for most other beverages in which caffeine has been removed. The absolute worst is sugar-free, caffeine-free, taste-free Dr Pepper. Water from a hoof print tastes better. At least it has some taste.

Then there are the instant "flavored" coffees with chocolate and mint and who knows what else blended in them. These might be fine for preppies or yuppies or any of the other "in" crowds these days, but they aren't real coffee. I want coffee that tastes like coffee, not like a melted after-dinner mint.

I like coffee that has some punch to it, that can practically walk to the table on its own. That's real coffee, not these weak sister substitutes that can barely get through the percolator on their own, or have to depend on additives for flavor. Coffee should be able to stand on its own. Literally.

Now, if you'll excuse me, I feel the urge for a coffee break coming on.

CHAPTER 68
WAITING TABLES, GOOD SER-
VICE AND MUTUAL RESPECT

Waiting on tables has got to be one of the toughest jobs in the world.

Just look at everything waitresses -- and waiters -- have to put up with every day. They're constantly on their feet and on the go. Like acrobats in the circus, they have to balance dishes, often hot ones, as they maneuver through tables filled with customers and past other servers, then they have to get the right order to the right people.

Good ones are constantly on the move as they take orders, serve orders, check on their customers, fill and refill drinks, make sure everyone gets what they ordered. Some make small talk with the customers as they wait on them, all the while keeping an eye on their other tables. I've recently encountered several excellent waitresses -- and waiters -- and been impressed by the services rendered. Theirs has been the "finest kind," to quote Hawkeye Pierce.

I respect waitresses -- and waiters -- and I appreciate the job the good ones do. They're the ones who are overworked, underpaid and often underappreciated. For their efforts they get sore feet, aching backs, headaches and assorted pains, some of which are regular customers. They deserve more than they get because they've earned it.

On the other side of the coin, I've encountered some waitresses -- and waiters -- who probably should consider a career change.

As I said, it's not an easy job, so I can understand why a server might not be at the top of his or her game every day. However, the trick is to not let the customer know it.

Good ones don't. No matter how bad things may be, they still do their jobs the way they should.

In the last few weeks, I've run into one waitress who seemed positively miserable with her very existence and cast a bleak shadow over our dining experience; another who was surlier than Jack Webb in *The D.I.* and had the people skills of Attila the Hun; a third to whom our very presence, nay, our existence, seemed to be an inconvenience; and yet another who, given her way, would not to this day have acknowledged us had not someone else pointed us out at her table.

Once again, that's not the norm. Most waitresses -- and waiters -- do a good job.

But it seems most people remember the bad service they get, and that's what they tell other people about. With the price of dining out these days, people rightfully expect good service, not service with a snarl, whether it's a sit-down restaurant with real plates and flat ware or a fast-food place with Styrofoam cartons and plastic forks. There's just something that galls me about paying the cost of a meal and being treated as if I'm disrupting some individual's life because I dare ask for a refill of iced tea.

It's also aggravating to have to wait 10 minutes before being acknowledged as a customer, then waiting another 20 minutes while the server apparently disappears into another realm of existence before taking your order. It's even more aggravating if you get that treatment while the server remains in full view, propped up on a counter, apparently memorizing her fingerprints while ignoring you and the only other customer in the whole joint.

I don't run into those situations very often, but when I do, they stand out in my memory and certainly affect the decision process when picking out a place to eat the next time, just as it does that of other people.

Fortunately, as I said, most of the servers I encounter are hard working, friendly and provide good service. They should be treated respectfully. Don't harangue them or be rude to them. They're just trying to make a living in a hard line of work. By the same token, they shouldn't be rude to customers or ignore us. We're just trying to get a meal. All of us should be able to meet in the middle to the benefit of all.

And to those who provide service par excellence, my hat's off to all of you waitresses and waiters.

CHAPTER 69
ONE BURGER, HOLD THE STYROFOAM

One of those fast-food places, after spending about a million dollars on research, has introduced a new item to its menu – the hamhamburger.

Of course, the chain had been selling hamburgers for years, but only after months of work did it discover the public has a taste for the noble hamburger with everything on it.

The fast-food chain that's introducing the hamburger to the American public also spent a few thousand bucks to determine what condiments people want on it, too. Researchers found lettuce, tomato, pickle and onion go well on hamburgers. I always thought that was supposed to be on a hamburger.

Some places actually charge extra for lettuce and tomato on burgers. That's like buying a Buick and finding out the transmission and wheels are options.

Ketchup also is included on the new hamburgers, which is something I could do without. It appears ketchup was meant to be a substitute for to-matoes on burgers. A bun, a piece of meat and a dollop of ketchup and mustard served in Styrofoam do not a burger make.

I grew up eating hamburgers and their cele-brated cousins, cheeseburgers. On each and every one of them, the lettuce, tomato, pickle and onion were standard equipment, not options. You didn't have to ask that it be added. If you didn't want any of them, you simply asked the waitress to hold the onion or whatever you didn't want.

Some of the best hamburgers and cheeseburg-ers I've ever encountered came from a little café called The Roundtable. It was a small place, with round tables as well as the customary vinyl booths, just off the East Texas State University campus at Commerce, Texas. It was a haven for us students, a place to meet, eat and study from early in the morning until late at night. We solved more than our share of the world's problems there over burgers, fries and coffee.

The Roundtable served up burgers that were manna from heaven for hungry college students. These were the kind hamburger lovers dreamed about. The buns were as big around as a salad plate, toasted as a bun should be, and there defi-nitely was more burger than bun. Heaped on the patty was crisp green lettuce, juicy red tomato slices, sweet white onion slices and pickles that snapped when bitten. It came with both mustard and mayonnaise.

For the more hearty diner, there were double-burgers available. After eating a double, you didn't need to eat for about two days. You could get a burger basket with French fries that made what you get at some places now look like toothpicks. If you got it to go, the burger was wrapped like hamburgers should be in wax paper, which absorbed the juices and grease. Hamburgers weren't meant to be put in boxes.

And the price was just right. For under $2, you could get a piece of paradise on toasted buns.

I haven't been back to Commerce for a long time, so I'm not sure of The Roundtable is still there, or if it still serves the best burger in the world. I hope it hasn't fallen victim to the age of fast-food instant burgers and salad bars, which I fear may eventually take over the world.

Since I graduated from ETSU, I haven't come across a burger to equal that of The Roundtable's. There was a place in Texarkana that came close, but there just was something a little extra special about those offered at The Roundtable.

Despite their best efforts, and no matter how tasty they might be, I don't think the new hamburgers served by fast-food chains will ever equal those of my college days.

CHAPTER 70
A TASTE OF CHICKEN

"What's that?"

"I'm not sure, but it tastes like chicken."

How often have you heard that? No matter what something may be, it always seems to taste like chicken. This especially is so whenever the conversation turns toward any exotic fare.

For example, one of our friends recently sampled alligator at a local eating establishment. What did it taste like?

"Chicken."

Another individual I know agreed that alligator tastes like chicken, "only chewier."

When the conversations turns on the hub of exotic or unusual food, the subject of eating snake tends to arise. I haven't sampled that particular bit of reptilian fare. There's just something about dining on a creature that slithers …

It seems the type of snake doesn't matter because folks usually say it tastes like, you guessed it, chicken.

"Greasy chicken," was the comment I heard the other day.

OK. There's nothing wrong with alligator and snake tasting like chicken, but it seems to me any other unusual meat that is offered is said to taste like chicken.

"Here, try this fried parrot."

"What does it taste like?

"Chicken."

"Take a bit of this stewed sloth.

"What does it taste like?"

"Chicken."

You see what I mean?

If it's not your typical, farm-raised, protein-laden, run-of-the-mill meat, those urging others to sample it insist it tastes like chicken.

I wonder what the first person who tried chicken compared it with when serving it to guests at the dinner table for the first time?

"What is this stuff?"

"It's called chicken."

"What's a chicken?"

"You know, it's a bird that scratches around the barnyard, eats gravel and whatever else it finds on the ground and lays eggs.

"I'm not eating that."

"Oh, it's good. Go ahead and try it."

"Not me."

"Really, go ahead. It tastes like, uh … well, it's sort of like …Hmmmmmmm, it's got a flavor similar to …"

"What does it taste like?"

"Well, it's hard to describe. It's not like cow or lamb or fish, but some of it's white like fish."

"So this strange bird tastes like fish?"

"Not exactly."

"Does it taste like pork chops?"

"No, it doesn't taste like pork chops."

"How about ham?"

"No, it doesn't taste like ham, either."

"Look, I'm not eating this if you don't know what it tastes like."

"It's really not that bad, especially with all these herbs and spices."

"Well, what do they taste like?

"Herbs and spices."

"Right. Look, just pass me some of those vegetables and a little of that fruit, and you keep the bird. Say, what's that over there?"

"These? They're frog legs."

"What do they taste like?"

"Oh, they taste like chicken."

CHAPTER 71
YES, FRIENDS, WE ALMOST
HAVE NO BANANAS

F orget chemical weapons in Iraq. The heck with nuclear development in North Korea. Who cares about the economy? The world's running out of bananas, and that's a real crisis.

I just learned of the impending extinction of the banana Friday when the Netscape home page popped up with a CNN story about the problem.

According to the story, New Scientist magazine reported that Emile Frison, head of the International Network for the Improvement of Banana and Plantain, broke the news that the banana could disappear within 10 years. Besides the fact the banana is a sterile, seedless fruit, Frison said it lacks enough genetic diversity to fight off diseases and pests.

Apparently the only way to save the banana is through biotechnology and genetic manipulation. Otherwise, banana production could decline and eventually disappear.

It's hard to imagine the banana going the way of the dinosaur, the dodo bird and the liberal Republican. "Extinction" and "banana" shouldn't even be in the same sentence.

This could be a tremendous tragedy for the world. After all, the banana is one of the most-loved fruits in the world. People everywhere enjoy the soft, sweet fruit, from infants with no teeth to seniors with no teeth.

Without bananas, we couldn't have banana pudding, banana bread, banana daiquiris. There would be no banana chips, banana dips, banana flips. We wouldn't have banana ice cream, banana splits or Bananas Foster.

Can you imagine a world without banana cream pie or strawberries and bananas? And where would we be without chocolate-covered bananas and Funky Monkeys?

Oh, friends, what would we do without bananas? Hikers, backpackers and extreme sports enthusiasts would have nothing to put in their packs to mash then eat. School children wouldn't have anything to turn brown in their lunch sacks. Mothers wouldn't have anything to set on kitchen counters and watch as it changes from green to yellow to brown.

And what about comics? Where would they be without banana peel jokes and pratfalls? In movies, what else could drape so well over characters' heads when they rise up from trash dumpsters?

Yes, this is a serious crisis. We may have to permit banana cloning to preserve the fruit. If science can make sheep, then scientists should be able to bioengineer bananas.

They could even develop a superbanana -- bigger, tastier, yellower.

This is not something we can take lying down. In a world where people fight to preserve the snail darter, the spotted owl, the Ozark big-eared bat, the manatee, the arroyo toad and Attwater's greater prairie chicken, surely people will rally around the beloved banana.

I, for one, promise to be among that number. We can't have a world without bananas.

Save the banana!

CHAPTER 72
WATERMELONS: THE TRUEST SIGN OF SUMMER

I'd drive an hour and a half for a Cave City watermelon. In fact, that's just what we did last weekend when we made our annual pilgrimage to Cave City to get some of the finest melons you ever tasted.

Hope, down in southwest Arkansas, can brag about its huge watermelons, but size isn't everything. I've run across some big melons that were as tasteless as cardboard, but I've never found one of any size from Cave City that wasn't good.

Every August, we get some Cave City melons. For the last couple of years, friends and relatives who know we're making a watermelon run have put in their order. This year, we hauled back 20 watermelons -- 16 red and four yellow.

There's something about watermelons that just make summer summer. Few things refresh you as much as sweet, juicy watermelon when the temperature soars. Whether plain or with a little sprinkle of salt to enhance the flavor, it just can't be beat.

I'll eat both red- and yellow-meated melons. Some folks don't care for the yellow ones; they don't look like watermelons. But it doesn't matter to me. While we were visiting our friends Myrtle and Don, we got some yellow watermelon. With its golden color and sugary taste, it was like eating honey.

Getting watermelon is one of my favorite things about summer. When I was a youngster running around with cousins and friends in sandy fields in northeast Texas, we could hardly wait when watermelons were ready. When my family picked watermelons to take home, one or two would inevitably wind up hitting the ground and breaking open.

Accidentally, of course.

Since there was no sense in letting perfectly good melons go to waste, we youngsters would plunge our grubby little hands into the juicy red fruit and yank out huge bites. Sometimes the grownups would get into it, too.

There we'd be, sitting on the ground, watermelon juice rolling off our chins and running down our arms, with huge grins covering the parts of our faces that weren't covered in watermelon.

That's the way a youngster should eat watermelon. Just crack it open and dive in, casting manners to the wind.

As for the proper etiquette for disposing of watermelon seeds, well, there's the genteel method of picking them out with a fork while cutting off bites of melon. Much more fun is just biting off chunks of melon, squirreling away the seeds in your cheeks as you chew, then, after swallowing, seeing how far you can spit them.

Naturally this is more practical outside.

I've been trying to grow watermelons this year, and so far they've done well. From a pile of creek dirt and garden builder, six plants have produced a giant tangle of vines with several melons. They're nowhere near the size of Hope melons, or even Cave City melons, but they're big enough.

A couple cracked open, apparently because of the heat, and while not totally ripe, enough had turned red to sample, and they weren't bad. Now if the rest will just get ripe before the heat gets to them.

I've been thinking about saving seeds from our Cave City melons and planting them next. I know it's the soil that makes the melon, but with a little luck I might get close to growing an almost-Cave City watermelon.

Of course, we'd still have to make that trip to Cave City next August to get the genuine article.

CHAPTER 73
HOW DO YOU LIKE THAT SANDWICH, PARTNER?

I'm anxious to see the new movie *The Four Feathers*, which features former Mountain Home resident Wes Bentley in a featured role.

I didn't know the young actor when he lived here. In fact, according to his biography, he was born the year I moved to Mountain Home, so we probably didn't have a lot in common.

Still, it is kind of exciting to realize someone up on the big screen is a hometown boy or girl, or that you can say, "I know him."

Probably the next best thing is getting to meet a celebrity. One of the benefits of this job is that you sometimes get to meet well-known people. It falls in what I call the "Beaver Cleaver Category" when I describe newspaper work -- sometimes you get to see and do some really neat stuff. In this case, meeting famous people. Sure, journalists meet and interview politicians, officials, industrial bigwigs and such all the time. But how many can say they've gotten a menu recommendation from Ben Johnson?

(You remember Ben Johnson, cowboy actor, generally played grizzled characters, won the Oscar for *The Last Picture Show*.)

Or visited with Iron Eyes Cody? (You remember Iron Eyes Cody, acted in several westerns, was the Indian with the tear in the anti-litter commercials, co-starred with Jim Varney in *Ernest Goes to Camp*.)

I got to meet both of them when I was working at Texarkana. They were in town along with Lana Wood (Natalie Wood's sister) Jack Elam and Dub Taylor to help promote the Charles B. Pierce epic *Grayeagle*.

Pierce had been Mayor Chuckles, the host of an afternoon TV cartoon show, then started making movies. His first was *Legend of Boggy Creek*, a docudrama about the Fouke monster, whose stomping grounds were near Texarkana. He went on to make several B-movies, including *The Town That Dreaded Sundown* (about Texarkana's infamous Phantom Killer mystery) and *The Norseman* (which starred Lee Majors as a Viking).

Anyway, Pierce brought several cast members from *Grayeagle* to Texarkana for a premiere showing. Now, you've got these character actors -- Johnson, Elam, Taylor, Cody -- who usually play pretty tough characters sitting around before a news conference. What were they talking about?

Sandwiches.

OK. Tough guys have to eat, too, and they probably were looking for some place that had manly dining. Maybe thick steak sandwiches, or barbecue sandwiches with meat stacked so high you could barely get the sandwich in your mouth.

Nope.

Ben Johnson -- Academy Award winner, a real cowboy who became an actor and whose characters usually didn't take guff off anyone -- recommended the hotel's Monte Cristo sandwich.

A Monte Cristo sandwich?

Ben Johnson said it was one of the best he'd ever had.

He'd eaten more than one Monte Cristo sandwich in his life?

The Monte Cristo sandwich served in the hotel restaurant had thinly sliced ham and turkey with cheese between two slices of bread that were dipped into beaten eggs and grilled like French toast. Then powdered sugar was sprinkled over it and the sandwich was served with marmalade.

Tough guy Ben Johnson -- who co-starred with John Wayne, Charlton Heston, Charles Bronson -- ate Monte Cristo sandwiches, something that sounded as if it were more suitable for a ladies' afternoon tea party than a two-fisted cowboy.

Sometimes in this job you learn things you'd just as soon not know.

Ben Johnson also didn't like to cuss on screen, although he sometimes had to. He said his mother didn't like it.

OK, he was a tough guy actor with a soft spot for his mom. I guess that makes up for liking a sissy sandwich.

I wonder what kind of sandwich Wes Bentley likes? Of course, it might be best to not know.

CHAPTER 74
THE JOYS OF CATFISH

A recent government survey – and who's better at surveys than the government – shows that catfish sales soared last year as they climbed 17 percent to claim a $285 million market. Who would have thought five years ago that the lowly catfish, that river bottom scavenger, would become so popular?

Down South, we've always known about the joys and delights of catfish. It's one of the national foods of the South and a favorite of Southerners no matter how far they roam from home. Just throw a few cornmeal-battered catfish steaks into a pot of hot oil anywhere in the South, and before the heavenly aroma's barely drifted away on the breeze you'll be surrounded by folks holding out their plates.

Why, some youngsters go from the bottle right to catfish, after it's been carefully deboned, of course. There's nothing more aggravating than getting a fish bone, cat or other, caught somewhere between your tonsils and your Adam's apple.

There was a time when you didn't often find catfish outside the South and its border states. A lot of folks just didn't care for the appearance of the catfish. I'll admit it's uglier than the Ayatollah. In fact, aside from a few exotic breeds of fish, the catfish undoubtedly is one of the ugliest creatures to plum the waters of the Earth.

But catfish are meant for eating, not winning beauty pageants. And even though it's a fine-tasting fish, many people still have been reluctant to eat what they think is the aquatic equivalent of a buzzard. True, catfish are your basic scavengers who keep river and lake bottoms clean, but they still taste good. Especially with a few hushpuppies, some slaw, a helping of green tomato pickles and a big, sweet onion slice.

A few years ago, somebody got the bright idea to start raising catfish in ponds instead of just catching them out of rivers and lakes. And instead of letting the fish eat whatever they found, the fish farmers fed them corn. That helped open a few more doors for this southern delicacy. It also eliminated that sometimes-muddy taste you got, particularly with river cats.

Cattle, hogs and sheep eat corn before they become steaks, ham and chops, so someone thought it would help catfish with reluctant diners. And it did. Before you knew it, Yankees were chowing down on catfish as if they'd just invented it.

Since a lot more people have begun eating fish for their health, the catfish's popularity continues to climb. Unfortunately, the best way of cooking cat-fish – deep-frying – makes nutritionists and health fanatics cringe. So fancy-pants chefs started looking for new ways to fix the old favorite.

Now you can find recipes for blackened catfish (which doesn't strike me as that much of an im-provement over you basic frying), broiled catfish, baked catfish, catfish with cream sauce and catfish almandine. Just about the only think it's being used for is catfish sushi, although I once had some un-dercooked catfish that almost qualified.

Some of these modern ways of catfish prepara-tion don't sound too bad, although it's still hard to beat your basic fried catfish dinner. Give me a plateful of catfish and all the trimmings, and I'm in heaven. Why, I bet even the Good Lord likes catfish and hushpuppies every now and then.

CHAPTER 75
CHEESEBURGERS AS HEALTH FOOD

I n the process of getting caught up with the rest of the world after a week of shuttling back and forth to Harrison, I finally found a bit of good news. Actually, I think it potentially could be the biggest news item of the week

It's not the Ollie North trial, nor the Alaskan oil spill, and not even the opening of baseball season, all of which certainly are important to the future. No, friends, the big story this week is the news that cheeseburgers may be good for us.

This announcement comes after years of listening to researchers, nutritionists, doctors, health food advocates, vegetarians and others warn us against eating such fare. How often have we been told that beef and cheese will clog our arteries, damage our systems and generally ruin our health?

Don't forget, many of these were the same folks who essentially advocated the Yogi Bear diet – meals of nuts and berries.

Now, we still have to watch cholesterol and the fats that are found in a cheeseburger, but now we can eat one without guilt. We also can enjoy cheeseburgers without the feeling those around us are looking disdainfully at us with raised eyebrows and healthier-than-thou attitudes.

But this week we hear from researchers that there's an acid, CLA, in cheeses and broiled beef that can act as an anti-carcinogen and may help ward off cancer. Various cheese and cheese products were listed as having high CLA content, including two of my favorites, Roquefort and blue cheese.

Actually, the top of the list is Cheez Whiz. You know, the cheese in a glass jar that you can pop in the microwave and nuke into sauce and dip in a matter of seconds. This is the cheese that comes in cans and you can squeeze it onto crackers, celery, melba toast and even directly into your mouth.

Can you imagine what the reaction must have been when those who would have us all chewing tofu and bean curds heard Cheez Whiz may be good to use? I bet they thought, "No whey."

And they really must have lost it upon learning eating beef, second on the list, could be healthy. If some of those folks had their ways, we'd have to find a new purpose for using cattle since eating them would be out of the question.

Fortunately, this group of researchers comes along with the word that, in moderation, broiled lean beef and cheese – two key ingredients in cheeseburgers – can be good for our health. I wouldn't be one bit surprised to see Burger King, with its flame-broiled burgers, promoting itself as a healthy alternative to those other fast-food places.

And we'll probably see more promotions for cheeseburgers than we've ever seen before. After all, when it was suggested oat bran was good for us, we were inundated with more oat bran products than we knew what to do with.

It's nice to learn that during all the years I've been eating cheeseburgers that I've also been introducing plenty of CLA into my system, and there's been something healthy about my eating habits.

I've always thought cheeseburgers had a special place in the universe, especially after discovering the cheeseburgers at the Roundtable in Commerce, Texas years ago. Now, that belief has been confirmed scientifically.

Throw a little lettuce, tomato, pickles and onion on toasted whole-wheat buns, and you've got a healthy selection of vegetables to go with the beef and cheese, although I'd go lightly with any mustard and mayonnaise. Nobody's said that's good for us. Yet.

Ah, yes, as Jimmy Buffett would say, "Cheeseburger is paradise."

Now, if researchers can just find a way to prove fries and chocolate shakes are healthy …

CHAPTER 76
IN DEFENSE OF FRUITCAKES

You've got to feel sorry for fruitcakes – the ones people give each other this time of year, not the ones who usually run for office.

A poll this week put fruitcakes at the very top of the least-favorite Christmas gifts. Someone even theorized there may be only one fruitcake in the world, and it keeps changing hands because nobody wants it. Those quizzed in this survey had a variety of reasons for disliking fruitcake, from its taste to its appearance.

Now, honestly, what's wrong with fruitcake?

Sure, some of them have an unusual flavor with all those candied fruits and nuts blended together. And some even look funny, if not downright odd. But there's nothing wrong with them.

Even Eli likes the red and green cherries that come off fruitcakes. So do I, although I'm a little suspicious of the citron. Actually, I'm not certain what citron is and whether it comes from a tree or a bush or some place I'd just as soon not know about.

THOMAS GARRETT

Since I like to dabble in the kitchen every now and then, I've even tried my hand at making fruit cakes a couple of times. While it's true you could have used them to fill a College Street pothole, I didn't really think they turned out half bad. At least I never heard of anyone succumbing from eating any of them.

Personally, I prefer the ones with more fruit and nuts than batter. A truly good fruitcake has just enough cake to hold the fruit together -- no more, no less. And, while some will disagree, the best ones I've come across came from Texas, where a couple of towns claim to be the fruitcake capitals of the world. (I'll let that last line pass without additional comment.)

Still, there have to be worse gifts to give at Christmas than a fruitcake. Why, I can think of several gifts that could be worse than a fruitcake. For example, a moose head with glow-in-the dark antlers and a red electric nose would be a pretty tasteless gift.

Things like an all-expenses paid trip to any location where there's an abandoned nuclear facility and a year's reserved seating at Mountain Home City Council meetings probably would make fruitcake seem like an entirely appropriate expression of feelings.

Yes, there are other gifts that could make fruit cakes appealing, such as:

- A collection of *Bill Clinton Nominating Speeches, Vol. 1*

- An album of *Zamfir Performs Slim Whitman's Greatest Hits.*
- An evening with Ned Reynolds and Wally Hall.
- A Roseanne Barr cheesecake poster.
- A video of *Andy Rooney's Greatest Hits.*
- An electric tire gauge.
- Neon green boxer shorts with little caricatures of Yasser Arafat.
- That brass Buddha with a clock in his belly that Aunt Mildred gave Cousin Ralph who gave it to Uncle Waldo who could find anyone else to give it to.

You get the idea.

So, when somebody gives you a fruitcake this holiday season, accept it with a smile and be thankful because it could be much worse. They could have given you a collection of *Bill Clinton Nominating Speeches, Vol. 2.*

CHAPTER 77
MEALS IN A THIMBLE

Since folks tend to follow the herd instinct in today's social trends, it's appropriate that grazing is the latest food fad.

Grazing, in this connotation, doesn't involve getting on all fours and munching on the St. Augustine in the front lawn, although some individuals think that probably would be healthier than meat and potatoes. No, grazing basically means instead of sitting down to a meal, we all sit down to appetizers.

It used to be when you went to a banquet they passed around appetizers while everyone visited and waited for the main dish to be served. Now, the appetizers are the main course.

Ever since the salad bar became the benchmark for sophisticated dining, the trend has been to slip away from meals and eat only the pre-meal offerings. Someone got the idea that the salad itself could be a meal, so restaurants and fast-food franchises started shoving lettuce at their customers as if they were rabbits. Now, a place isn't considered classy if it doesn't have lettuce, tomatoes, radishes and bean sprouts sitting in the middle of its dining room.

Then a light bulb flashed in someone's darkened mind, and the idea of eating appetizers instead of a meal escaped. Instead of a chicken dinner, we got tiny chicken parts, as one commercial so gleefully explained.

Other forms of food have been processed into parts, or nuggets, and are being served up with our choice of sauce, I still can't quite get used to the idea of beef nuggets. Where I come from, beef doesn't have nuggets.

True, grazing does give one an opportunity to sample different foods at one sitting. You can combine an assortment of appetizers and make a meal of them much easier than combining many entrees to create indigestion. A little of this, a little of that, and, before you know it, you've created a mini-smorgasbord of finger food.

I've partaken of the grazing trend and found the offerings of some food bars superior to others' entire menus. But what I really wonder about is the move to shrink the size of food. One fast-food chain is advertising cheeseburgers the size of poker chips. Another offers chicken sandwiches you can carry in your watch pocket.

These things aren't even large enough to qualify as appetizers. It's like the places that believe six chicken nuggets are sufficient for a meal. Six chicken nuggets are the start of a meal, not the finish. A burger I can hide in my hand isn't likely to curb my appetite.

If this trend toward tinier tidbits persists, there's no telling where it could end. We could someday find ourselves sitting down to a three-course meal with all three courses served simultaneously on a saucer. A formal banquet could become a Swedish meatball and a Ritz.

Of course, restaurants also could save money since they wouldn't need as much space. They could operate out of phone booths and reconditioned Volkswagen vans. Since entire meals could be held in the palm of your hang, there would be no need for tables and chairs, and that's another expense they could save.

All this talk of food is making me a little hungry. So, if you'll excuse me, I thin I'll wander down to my favorite watering hole and graze a bit. I hear the bean sprout and chicken parts miniburger is fresh today.

(As in most things, the pendulum swung, and these days it's gone the other way with food being supersized to the point one burger can feed a family of four.)

CHAPTER 78
A HOT TOPIC

Being from Texas originally, and having had a close, lifelong personal relationship with spicy food, I naturally read with interest a little news item about the link between chili peppers and pain.

Anyone who has unsuspectingly, or unwittingly, chomped down on a jalapeno or other hot pepper knows almost all there is to know about the link between chili peppers and pain. The same is true of folks who have dipped their chip into a bowl and scooped up a mouthful of thick salsa only to discover they could have achieved the same results by munching a hot coal as an appetizer.

I recall such an encounter once at the Spanish Kitchen in Corpus Christi. In these parts, I'd gotten used to the green sauces being the mild variety and had allowed myself to be lulled into a false sense of security. With tortilla chip in hand, I proceeded to place the equivalent of about half a tablespoon of ground green pepper into my mouth. Too late, I realized it was nothing but jalapeno.

THOMAS GARRETT

Noticing the smoke rising from my ears and seeing that my face was the color of a fire truck, the
waitress brought a large quantity of ice water to our
table. Without even being asked. She received an
above-average tip for her excellent service.

Following that line of thought, don't forget
about those poor folks who handle jalapenos or
other hot peppers, then forget to wash their hands.
They are among those who understand pain. Such
forgetfulness can contribute to a great deal of pain
later should you rub your eyes, or pick your nose, or
touch other … sensitive areas.

However, the story – datelined form that bastion
of chili peppers, Newark, N.J. – dealt with the effect
chili peppers have on our ability to detect pain. According to research conducted by Rutgers University and a Mexican counterpart, they found eating
lots of chili peppers may lower sensitivity to pain.

Anyone who has ever experienced the afore-
mentioned situations can attest to that discovery.
Putting a heap of homegrown fire on our tongue
does tend to make it somewhat less sensitive. Of
course, it's also difficult to taste or feel anything
else when you have a mouth full of seared flesh.

But, back to the news.

Those folks involved in the study spent a lot of
time and effort examining the effects of capsaicin,
the stuff that makes peppers what they are, on labo-
ratory rats. Reading between the lines of the wire
service dispatch, it appeared these researchers gave
large quantities of capsaicin to the rats.

It didn't mention if the researchers offered the rats a cold Lone Star longneck or even a Corona afterwards.

When the scientists discovered that giving rats large quantities of capsaicin was that capsaicin apparently destroys some pain-related nerves. Shoot, in the right quantity it probably could destroy cities and level forests. What the wire service dispatch didn't mention, however, was whether scientists considered the capsaicin-induced destruction of the nerves good news or bad.

I suppose if your diet included enough chili peppers and capsaicin to make you unaware your hair was on fire it could be considered bad news. On the other hand, these folks might have discovered a new anesthetic that might be more pleasant than any injection you might receive.

Of course, serving large amounts of salsa and tortilla chips before surgery could prove a little messy in the operating theater.

It will be interesting to see where these discoveries take researchers. It hasn't been confirmed yet, but it is rumored they may look into the possibility that large amounts of chili con queso can clear the sinuses.

CHAPTER 79
FINDING A HICKORY-SMOKED TASTE OF HEAVEN

I f you haven't guessed by now, I enjoy good food.

I enjoy a variety of food. I'm usually willing to try something new, unless it involves giant larvae or rosemary. I'd probably take the giant larvae over the rosemary.

I've been stung one too many times with food seasoned with rosemary. Usually it seems the cook goes overboard with it, and instead of getting a hint of "woody" flavor it tastes as if it were marinated in a half-cup of Pine-Sol.

Other than that, I enjoy most foods. People who make big and tall clothing are happy that I enjoy most foods, although in my case the tall is just a waste of time.

Anyway, one of my favorite foods is barbecue, or barbeque, or BBQ, or bar-b-q, or however you want to spell it. Being raised in Texas and having spent my life south of the Mason-Dixon Line, barbecue was as much a part of my upbringing as going to vacation Bible school every summer and learning to say "ma'am" and "sir" when spoken to by an elder.

Through the years, I've sampled a wide array of barbecue. Some of it has been excellent, some fair and some just has been downright awful. I've been to more than one restaurant that claimed renown for its barbecue only to be served lunchmeat with spicy ketchup.

I kid you not. One place Kim and I ate tried to pass off what amounted to thick-sliced canned ham as "delicious, slow-smoked Ozark ham." It was lunchmeat with spicy ketchup.

At another establishment their idea of barbecue involved apparently boiling the fattiest portion of pork they could find and soaking it with tomato sauce and chili powder. Fortunately, their portions were small.

Barbecue is something that has to be done right. There aren't any shortcuts. Dad was a barbecue lover and always on the lookout for good barbecue. He was even more particular than I am. If he got stung once on a place's barbecue, there was no second chance. Offend his taste buds, offend the man.

Dad could do a fairly good job of making his own barbecue. He liked using chunks of hickory when he could, burned down to just the right amount of heat and smoke, and he took his time. After all, cooking barbecue slowly is the key. You can't rush barbecue. Most of what I know about barbecue I learned from Dad.

A VIEW FROM THE HILLS

Back in DeKalb, there was a man named Bobby on what was then referred to as the "colored" side of town who had a little barbecue joint. It was a cinder-block building big enough for a small kitchen and a counter where you could place your order. A barbecue plate consisted of your choice of meat, potato salad, slaw, beans, a slice of Wonder bread and, if you wanted, a jalapeno.

His smoker was out back, and there he worked magic with ribs, pork, brisket and chicken. With low heat, hickory smoke (sometimes a little pecan wood) and knowledge only he had, Bobby turned these plain pieces of meat into something wonderful. Dad loved Bobby's barbecue. So did Mom and I. So did many of the people in DeKalb.

Sundays after church, cars and pickups from the other side of town lined the street by Bobby's place, and folks lined up at the little cinder-block building for his barbecue. They'd had a taste of salvation that morning; they wanted to follow it with a taste of heaven. And Bobby delivered.

That was the best barbecue I'd had. I've eaten Texas barbecue, Kentucky barbecue, various forms of southern barbecue, Memphis-style and Kansas City-style barbecue, yet it never compared to Bobby's. Most of it was good, but not like his.

I have found a place that not only brings back memories of that barbecue; I think it surpasses it. Now, in the interest of peace, I won't mention any names here, but the folks who run it know who they are, know I brag about them, and so do a lot of other people. Not only is their barbecue made the way it should be, it hits the right taste buds and brings back good memories for me. And I know Dad would have enjoyed it, too.

You know, in looking back over this I'm starting to get a craving for barbecue. I think I hear some ribs calling my name. Thank goodness there's no rosemary on them.

(If you want to sample the best barbecue in the Ozarks, and most any place else, stop by KT's on U.S. 62 in downtown Gassville, Ark.)

CHAPTER 80
RISE OF THE MACHINES
WELCOME TO THE
COMPUTER AGE

(I wrote this in 1983, not realizing it was just the opening phase of what would become a lifelong struggle between me and modern technology.)

This column started out to be about something completely different. However, modern technology kept raising its ugly head and devouring, in one fashion or another, that pulsating prose.

Anyone who has visited our confines here at Seventh and Hickory will have noticed our old typewriters have given way to modern, up-to-date, state-of-the-art computers and VDTs. The latter, for those who don't know – or don't particularly care – are video display terminals, devices which amount to portable Sonys connected to typewriter keyboards.

Yes, these marvels of technical achievement can do almost anything, from enabling us to write the stories you so anxiously await to letting us know the latest happenings in Outer Mongolia.

Unfortunately, that's not all they do.

Around here, our VDTs have been called everything except what they are on occasion.

No, actually they've been called everything except what they are every day. And some of those names involve a heritage impossible for a computer to have.

You see, it used to be the only way a story got lost around here as if it were misplaced or found its way into the jungle of year-old papers and notes on my desk. Now, thanks to computerization, we have a wealth of ways to lose stories.

At any given second, any of our six little devils – one of the milder names given these infernal contraptions – can decide in some warped, perverted microchip fashion to act on its own. Besides the minor, although frustrating, malfunctions, their worst habit is devouring stories. Either we haven't hit the right key or haven't fed our terminals the proper amount of electricity or have done something to offend them.

Whatever the reason, in less time than you can comprehend, the story about Sunday's church social or the Moose Lodge's latest dinner vanishes somewhere in the twilight zone. Sometimes, it may return, but more often it is eternally lost, only Rod Serling knows where.

The terminal I'm using to write this column, for example, is borrowed from our sports editor. As I prepared to write on my own VDT, it began mal-functioning. Actually, it seemed to be having a nervous breakdown.

At certain crucial moments, such as when I'm about to finish a column, the terminal becomes a critic and vaporizes it before my very eyes. Or, as another example, the story on the display screen suddenly gives way to a set of hieroglyphics not even the pharaohs' scribes could translate. It flashes, it quivers, it jumps sort of like Jell-O mixed with Mexican jumping beans. Then, it fades to black like the end of a poorly produced science fiction movie.

Mine is not the only one to have such traumatic experiences. The one I'm using now has a neat little trick of fading out at inopportune times, playing a computerized version of hide-and-seek. Another of our reporters has one which sometimes behaves ir-rationally, but whose favorite trick is buzzing at a decibel frequency just under that which turns ear-drums to guacamole.

Almost anyone who has ever worked with a computer can tell you tales of horror. Such as … wait a minute. I think the computer doesn't like what I'm saying.

It's … it's … turning on me.

It's beginning to glow.

I think it's about to …

CHAPTER 81
THE GREEN BOMB

I saw "Christine" at the Saturday matinee last week. It's the story of a '58 Plymouth Fury with a will all its own. It sort of reminded me of my own car, the Green Bomb.

While Christine is out to get anyone who offends it or its owner, the Green Bomb, a '76 Chevrolet Nova, sometimes seems to be out just to get its owner.

I've had the Green Bomb for seven years. I acquired it after its predecessor left me sitting on an interstate near Texarkana late one cold, rainy Friday night in December. Since the necessary repairs would have cost more than the car was worth, it was time to get another car.

It was love at first sight when I saw the Green Bomb sitting on the car lot. The price was reasonable – about half the cost of cars half its size today – and soon a deal was struck. As I came tooling up to my parents' house, the first thing my mother said was, "It's green."

It was bright green, a green to inspire the Irish in your soul, a green to put any emerald to shame. Thus, the Nova acquired its name.

The Green Bomb and I have had a fairly good relationship. It's usually gotten me where I want to go, and to some places I didn't want to go. Together, we once made an almost-record trip from the South Texas coast to my hometown. All told, the Green Bomb and I have traveled nearly 76,000 miles together.

In that time, it's picked up a few dents and dings, unfortunately. Someone decided to make a left turn through the Green Bomb's right front fender. Another time, some unidentified individual put a dent in the driver's door. The worst offense, which I must own up to, was denting the hood and poking a pole through the right front fender. Bumping an immovable object with an automobile with a fiberglass front end can create a hole in the car. And there have been times when the Green Bomb's gone a while between washings.

All these little things have added up through the years, as has the cost of repairing them. Now, the Green Bomb seems to be seeking revenge.

In the past year, the Green Bomb has had many flats, not from running over anything, but from the air apparently evaporating in the tires. I've lost count of how many there have been. The most recent was last week, while the spare was being repaired. It just knelt down in the parking lot like a runner with nowhere to go. The Green Bomb seemed to grin, as though to say, "Gotcha, turkey."

Another of its tricks – which can easily be remedied – involves the heater. You can be driving along with the heater on, blowing warm air, when suddenly the air becomes chilled, as though the Green Bomb is trying to tell me something. It's telling me to get a new thermostat.

Yet, there still is one embarrassing trick up its exhaust pipe.

Whenever the weather turns cold, the Green Bomb's windshield wipers come on for no apparent reason. I've tried finding the cause, to no avail. Not even the switch will turn them off.

Oh, the wipers do stop after a while – when the Green Bomb decides the time is right. Then it turns them on again moments later.

Usually, it decides to turn on the wipers while we're driving. Surrounded by traffic. When there's not even a hint of rain in the forecast. When I will most look like an idiot.

And I'd swear it chuckles at me.

Still, I suppose the Green Bomb and I are stuck with each other, especially now since no one else would want it after reading this. I just hope the Green Bomb doesn't learn about this column. There's no telling what it might think of next.

CHAPTER 82
CHILLING EXPERIENCES

I've already talked about my dislike of unnaturally cold weather, but that seems to have done little good since we've just gotten over our second dose of winter. In the last two weeks, I've had two experiences, which have increased my distaste with some of this season's meteorological conditions.

The first occurred when it snowed two weeks ago. I don't mind snow too much. Actually, I sort of like snow, as long as it doesn't turn to ice.

This time, the snow was quite lovely as it settled over our fair community, there was no ice mixed in with the soft white flakes, and the ground looked like it had been covered with sugar. It had pretty much covered everything when I left work that night, but fortunately the roads weren't too bad. I can't say the same for the interior of my car, the Green Bomb.

As I started home, the defroster hadn't warmed up sufficiently, and the windshield kept getting covered with a fine mist. I'd wipe it away and keep driving, but I began to notice something unusual beginning to take place in the interior of the Green Bomb.

A fine white sheen began to appear on the black dashboard, and I felt something striking my face. It felt like snow. It was snow. It was snowing.

Inside my car.

And the windows were beginning to freeze – inside my car.

I've heard of such phenomena occurring in domed stadiums, but inside a Nova?

Apparently, the moisture in the air was taking on the consistency of the moisture outside the Green Bomb, and it was snowing inside the car.

I wasn't sure how to deal with this situation, since I didn't have any skis at hand, and I knew there were no Winter Olympic events for the interior of a Chevy. I kept fiddling with the defroster and heater controls, and, finally, it began to get warm.

The frost on the inside of the windows began to melt, and the blowing snow ceased. The Green Bomb had returned to normal, or at least normal for it.

When I told Kim what happened, she laughed, but it seemed to be the laugh of someone humoring a person who claimed to have seen a UFO. But my story was true.

My second encounter came after I left work this past Sunday, after ice had accumulated on everything that didn't move, and some things that did.

I'd managed to make it from the office to the entrance of our subdivision. There, the ice-covered street refused to let me progress any further, like some guard who demanded the proper password before allowing you to pass.

The Green Bomb slipped and slid and wiggled on the skating rink surface of the road, but it wouldn't go forward. I backed up and tried again, to no avail. I gunned the car, but it still would not move any closer toward home.

I quickly discovered the only progress I was making was backwards and to the side, neither of which were directions in which I wanted to travel.

I continued my efforts as the Green Bomb did all it could to move forward, and we still got nowhere. Then, out of the cloud-filled night came an idea.

There was an old newspaper lying in the backseat. I placed different sections of it under the rear tires. Crossing my fingers – and my toes, just in case – I got back behind the wheel and hit the gas. The Green Bomb strained for a few seconds, then moved forward, its snow tires doing what they could to grip the road, and we were on our way.

Neither of these incidents have done anything to improve my opinion of winter conditions. From now on, give me my ice in a glass.

CHAPTER 83
IN THE COMPUTER WORLD

Sometimes I wonder if people who fear computers may someday take over the world aren't right. They've certainly taken over quite a bit of *The Bulletin*.

With all the changes in our paper, computers probably have brought one of the biggest internal changes to our cozy confines at Seventh and Hickory. It's been nearly two years since what you read in your paper came out of a typewriter. In fact, it's been nearly two years since I've even touched a real typewriter.

Today, everything here is done by Visual Display Terminals, and through "boxes" and "discs," more jargon for the electronic gizmos and whatchamacallits on the other side of our building.

These marvels of the computer age do everything except go to city council meetings for us, although I'm still trying to figure out a way to get mine to go in my place. ("Would someone please plug in *The Bulletin* reporter?")

THOMAS GARRETT

Push one button here, another there, and presto ... chango ... alakazam, little bits of green light on screen become words in your newspaper.

Push the wrong button, however, and what you've written disappears somewhere over the rainbow.

Up until now, we at *The Bulletin* have been the only ones putting words into these machines. Now, persons tapping away in a little office somewhere else are writing stories that find their way into our computers. No, they're not being put there by conspirators lurking in the bushes. The new source of stories is the Associated Press.

AP stories quietly make the trip from their points of origin to Mountain Home and on into *The Bulletin*'s computers via a special phone line. All we have to do is push a button, and we can have a list of the latest wire stories at our fingertips.

In an instant, you can jump from congressional debates in Washington to turkey-calling contests in Yellville. Sometimes, however, it's difficult to discern the difference between the two.

Computerization has made much of the work easier, more efficient and faster, but it also has taken away some traditional aspects of newspaper work.

Not too many years ago, you could walk into a newsroom and be greeted by the clatter of typewriters. The wire machine usually sat in a corner or its own little cubicle, humming when there was nothing to report, and madly clattering away when it

332

passed along the latest world developments. Whenever something exceptionally important occurred, a bell on the machine rang incessantly to alert you. When the bell rang like this demanding immediate attention, you knew it was important, and your adrenalin pumped just a little faster.

Now, a newsroom can be as silent as an insurance office thanks to these VDTs. When something important comes in by wire, it's quietly added to a computer file without fanfare, without demands we immediately come see what has happened.

These advances are miraculous, and I look forward to those to come, but I'll still miss the old wire machines and the excitement that little bell could generate.

Computers rarely create adrenalin surges.

(Times certainly have changed since these words were written, as have computers, and even the newspaper business and the way wire news is transmitted. I haven't been near a typewriter in two decades, and I'm still amazed by what can be done with computers. I've also learned that, in the right circumstances, computers can, indeed, cause adrenalin surges.)

CHAPTER 84
WELCOME TO THE TELEPHONE ZONE

(This was written in 1986, not long after auto-mated telephone service arrived in Mountain Home.)

Meet Fred Finklehopper, an ordinary man hoping to take care of an ordinary task on an ordinary spring day. But Fred is about to discover there is nothing ordinary about ... The Telephone Zone.

Fred's journey began simply enough after he moved into his new house and went to see about having his telephone connected. From the outside, it appeared to be a brick office building like any other brick office building. But, once he approached the glass doors, Fred began to realize something was different. He couldn't see through the dark glass, and written on the door were the office hours: 10 a.m. until 10:15 a.m. Glancing at his Timex, Fred saw it was 10:04 a.m., so he opened the door and stepped into another dimension.

It was a small room, like an anteroom. But there were no other doors. Dim light made it difficult for Fred to see, but what he did see made him wonder what was happening. Before him, on the wall, were three telephones, -- a red one, a white one and a black one. There was no other person in the darkened room.

Fred approached a small counter with an even smaller window, through which a tiny amount of light escaped. A hand laid a telephone receiver on the counter and pointed to it before withdrawing. Fred picked up the receiver.

"Can I help you?" asked a strangely mechanical-sounding voice.

"Yes, I'd like to have my phone connected," replied Fred, suspecting nothing. As with the glass doors, he couldn't see through the window very well. He could only make out a silhouetted shape against the glass.

"Why?" asked the voice.

"Well, I'd like to be able to call other people, and so other people could call me," Fred answered.

"Communication," noted the voice. "You'll need to pick up the white phone."

"Can't you help me?" inquired Fred innocently.

"Pick up the white phone," ordered the voice as the hand reached out and touched the receiver. Both disappeared.

Fred, feeling somewhat nervous, thought he shouldn't argue, so he picked up the white phone.

"Can I help you?" asked a distant-sounding voice.

"I'd like to have my phone connected," said Fred again. He was beginning to worry now.

"Why?" asked the voice on the white phone.

Eyebrows raised in wonderment, Fred again explained why he wanted his phone connected. The white phone didn't reply. By now, he was getting anxious. It was quiet.

Too quiet, thought Fred.

"I cannot help you," the voice on the white phone said finally. "Pick up the red phone."

"Wait a minute," sand Fred anxiously. "I just want to get my phone connected. Can't I see someone?"

"Pick up the red phone."

Fred picked up the red phone.

"Can I help you?" asked an even more distant-sounding voice on the red phone.

Fred sighed and explained his purpose for the third time.

"That is not my department," said the voice.

"Whose department is it?" demanded Fred, his fear turning to aggravation.

"It is not mine. Pick up the black phone," the voice told him.

"Look, I'm tired of dealing with someone I can't see," said Fred. "I want to see someone now."

"You cannot see anyone. Pick up the black phone, if you want service," ordered the red phone.
No, I won't pick up the black phone!" shouted Fred. shouted Fred. "I'm tired of talking to disembodied voices. I want a real person!"

"Pick up the black phone," said the voice. "Or else."

Fred, visibly shake, picked up the black phone.

"Can I help you?" asked a voice that sounded as if it came from another dimension.

Fred, near tears, explained why he as there, one more time.

"I'm sorry. It is 10:15, and I cannot help you. Come back tomorrow," said the voice.

"All you need is my name and address. Can't you just take that down and send someone to install my phone?" pleaded Fred.

"It is too late. Come back tomorrow," said the voice.

"Will there be someone here I can talk to?" asked Fred.

"We will be here," was the reply.

"But, won't someone, a person I can see face-to-face, be here?" he asked.

"We will be here," was all the voice would ay. "Please deposit $5 and leave. Your time is up. Have a nice day."

The voice was replaced by a dial tone, a dial tone heard only by those who have entered ... The Telephone Zone.

CHAPTER 85
MECHANICAL DIFFICULTIES

(After the Green Bomb gave up the ghost, my next car was a Dodge, also green, which served as interim transportation until I got my Nissan pickup, which I still have 20 years later and occasionally use.)

Like my carpentry skills, my mechanical aptitude leaves something to be desired. Mainly, mechanical aptitude.

If it can't be tapped, thumped, tipped or threatened into working properly, it has a distinct edge on me. Oh, I can go through the motions of some mechanical jobs and replace parts I know need replacing. But I just haven't gotten the hang of deducting the exact cause of a mechanical problem, unless it's ridiculously obvious.

If you can't readily see what the problem is, I can't help you. I know which end of a ratchet to hold and how to replace an oil filter, but if it's any more complicated than that, I'm in trouble.

Wires that are visibly broken, lines and hoses with leaks, spark plugs with as much corrosion as the Andrea Dorea offer fairly obvious indications of the cause of problems.

The drive shaft falling out of your car usually is a very good indication of a mechanical problem, too. If you've never dropped your drive shaft, let me tell you that it gives you a nice adrenalin rush as you suddenly hear crashing sounds and realize your vehicle is suddenly losing power in the middle of traffic.

Fortunately, mine fell out next to a conveniently located convenience store, and I managed to coast onto its parking lot. Despite having a long, banged-up cylindrical object dangling beneath my Dodge, luck was with me this time.. Usually such things like this happen to me at places such as Push Mountain Road between Lone Rock and Big Flat in the middle of the night when it's raining.

At least this time there was a phone handy and a supply of Coca-Cola and any other refreshments on which to munch while waiting for help.

Help was Dad and Kim. Now, I may be prejudiced, but if my father can't get it running again, it doesn't need to be on the road. A dangling drive shaft presents a little more of a problem than having to replace a spark plug or adjust a carburetor, but to a man who once repaired and rebuilt tank, it's merely a minor inconvenience.

A little baling wire and twine usually is sufficient to lift such mechanical units so you can tow the vehicle to another location. But this time, it kept falling down. When it f ell the second time, it was easy enough to solve the problem.

We just took the drive shaft completely off so my car could be towed without it snagging the drive shaft on the road.

I sat in the Dodge to guide it while Dad pulled it with his car, and Kim helped navigate. In order to help steer my car, the engine had to be running and, thanks to a minor tune-up, it as running smoothly.

Actually, without the drive shaft my Dodge provided the smoothest, quietest ride it has ever given me. I just had to sit there, guide it so it didn't wander into oncoming traffic and occasionally tap the brake so it didn't run over Dad's car.

We made it home all right, encountering only one minor snag as we started up a slight incline. Much of the rest of the afternoon was spent trying to track down another drive shaft, which eventually was located.

While Dad kept my car overnight so he could work on it the next day, he loaned me his to drive to work. It's definitely a one-man car because only one man – Dad – can operate it without problems. I had to take extra care to not break two cars in one day.

Fortunately, everything came out all right. Dad replaced the drive shaft in nothing flat and had the Dodge soon running as smooth as a sewing machine instead of a jackhammer. It doesn't squeak as it goes down the road, shake like it has the DTs or make crude, rude and socially unacceptable sounds in traffic.

Now, if Dad could just figure out a way to turn it from a Dodge into a Lincoln.

CHAPTER 86
WHO SAYS WE DON'T COMMUNICATE ANY MORE?

I've reached a conclusion -- I hate cell phones.
Hate may be too harsh a term.
Let's just say I've grown to despise them.

Actually, there's nothing really wrong with cell phones themselves (I even have one). Except for those that burst into a musical interlude instead of ringing when someone calls. You know the ones I'm talking about.

You're sitting in a restaurant, quietly looking at the menu, when suddenly from the table next to you the *William Tell Overture* begins playing in a sharp, tinny tone that sounds as if the Big Flat Philharmonic Orchestra has been jammed into an imported pocket transistor radio. It's the cell phone hanging on some guy's belt, and he answers it with a speed that would have gotten him multiple gunshot wounds in a fast-draw competition.

Why is it folks who have those irksome little contraptions can't seem to answer them quickly? They let the darned things play out whatever melody they've programmed into their phones before answering their calls and force all of us around them to have to endure their impromptu musical interludes.

Whenever I hear one of those cell phones I have to resist the urge to snatch up the phone and hurl it into the nearest wall or body of water, whichever is closer. By the third time it happens, I'm resisting the urge to snatch up the phone's owner and hurl him into the nearest wall or body of water.

Anyway, as I said, there's really nothing wrong with cell phones themselves, except for those miniature stereo wannabes. They are useful tools and can come in handy. Many a stranded driver's been rescued from the roadside thanks to cell phones, and they've proven invaluable in many an emergency situation. And they're good for keeping in touch with whomever you need to stay in touch.

But do people have to stay in touch constantly?

I guess it started for me on my trip to Washington. Everywhere you went there were people using cell phones. On the Mall, at memorials, at the museums, at airports. If there were people present, they were talking into cell phones. I could understand the ones at the airports as they phone in their good-byes or call for rides or check in on business. It seemed virtually everyone had cell phones and was using them as they hurried through the terminals.

After I got back, I started noticing everywhere I went more and more people had cell phones jammed against their ears.

In restaurants.
At the grocery store.
In Wal-Mart.
Driving down the road.
Walking along the sidewalk.
At public meetings.

When I was in Hot Springs at the Arkansas Press Association convention a couple of weeks ago cell phones were as plentiful as the toadstools in my backyard after heavy rains.

During vacation, it seemed you couldn't walk into any store without finding people jabbering into their cell phones. At Springfield, I was in a bookstore and before I could get to the back of the shop I'd passed a woman who was answering her cell phone (it rang, thank goodness), a teen-ager calling home to see if she'd had any calls and some guy explaining that they'd jumped up and down on the truck's tailgate and everything seemed OK.

Enough, people!

Do you really need to phone home every time you change aisles in a bookstore? Is it necessary to call in reports of bodily functions as you check the tomatoes in the produce section? Can you not eat a meal in a public restaurant without having to carry on a phone conversation?

Have we reached the point where we just can't get along without constant digital and electronic communication with someone? Personally, I think some folks get inflated egos with their cell phones, and they feel they're so important they have to remain in perpetual communication with someone, anyone.

You can spot them easily. He's the one talking into a cell phone as he pulls into a parking space, the one gabbing on his cell phone as he gets out and walks down the sidewalk, the one who takes his phone away from his ear long enough to request a non-smoking table in a restaurant then resume his conversation, who prattles between soup and salad, who babbles incessantly between bites of his meal, who chatters into his cell phone over dessert and finally hangs up in time for coffee.

Then the *1812 Overture* blares from his hip, and he's off again! But only after it plays the first three stanzas.

As Charlie Brown would say:
AAAAAARRRRRRGGGHHHH!!!

CHAPTER 87
COMPUTER GAMES HAVE COME A LONG WAY

It's amazing how sophisticated some toys and games have become. A couple of computer games are more advanced than the entire computer department of East Texas State University was when I was there.

(Yes, we had computers when I was in college, but they fit in entire buildings and laptop was where you spilled your beer at the local pub.)

Seriously, you almost need a college degree just to read the instructions with some of these new computer and video games. A few of the role-playing games, where you play a particular character, have plots that make *The Lord of the Rings* seem like a Weekly Reader serial.

Some have animated graphics that are better than the special effects in movies. One that I like, Age of Empires, has an opening that Cecil B. DeMille would have been proud to claim. The Final Fantasy series, Star Craft, WarCraft and Diablo also have some dandy animated sequences.

These things have come a long way from the time not too many years ago when the only video game consisted of a white dot bounced between two electronic paddles.

There were computer games when I was at ETSU. As I recall, they'd been developed by a couple of what these days would be called geeks or nerds. Honestly, these were guys who wore pocket protectors, had tape on their glasses, cut their own hair, bathed only when necessary -- which wasn't too often to them -- and could build their own hand-held calculators, from scratch. They'd passed almost every science class there was, but kept having trouble getting through the basic requirements for graduation.

Anyway, they came up with a couple of games. One was called "Wampus" and was a role-playing game. The player made his way through a series of caves looking for the wampus before the wampus got him. The wampus was some sort of hideous critter you had to shoot with arrows or stab with a sword. However, there was nothing visual. You typed in directions or responses to questions and got a written message back on the computer monitor telling you if you'd gotten the wampus, or vice versa.

Think of it as a sort of radio version of video games -- you had to picture the action in your mind.

Another game was similar to some of today's games. You were the monarch of a country and you decided things such as how much grain to plant, how much gold to acquire, what the taxes would be, if your kingdom would attack a neighboring kingdom and so forth. There were lots of different scenarios. If you planted no crops, taxed the people to the hilt, took all the gold and started a war, you got a message that your subjects had rebelled, stormed your castle and executed you. Again, this was without visual aids, only typed messages between the player and the computer.

All that was processed through a building-sized computer on terminals that looked like ancient Philco television sets with electric typewriters attached. Now most of that can be handled in something about the size of your thumbnail contained in a hand-held Gameboy, complete with color animation.

Talk about progress. So, if your youngsters keep asking for video and computer games for Christmas, just be glad you don't need to construct a building to house them, or have a couple of smelly, hairy undergraduates to program them.

CHAPTER 88
KEEPING TRACK OF YOURSELF IN THE CYBER AGE

In those old World War II movies there almost inevitably was a scene in which a soldier who'd drawn guard duty would demand a password from someone approaching his position.

"Who won the 1937 World Series?"

"The Yankees."

"Pass, friend."

It was the same thing in movies about the Roaring '20s, where some flapper would knock on a speakeasy door and say:

"Joe sent me."

That was about the extent the average person had anything to do with passwords, unless you belonged to a fraternal organization or secret society. Now everybody has to have a password, PIN number (which is redundant) to do everything from banking to turning on a computer.

It can get confusing when you try to keep up with your passwords because we keep getting told to not duplicate them from one situation to another, and avoid anything that would be obvious to anyone wanting to sneak into your account or computer.

Even our phones here at Sixth and Hickory have passwords to get our voice mail, and every few months the phones tell us to change them. Now, my voice mail usually isn't something that demands a lot of security. I rarely get anything top secret.

Everywhere you turn these days you almost have to have a security clearance, whether it's to get $5 from an ATM or to check your e-mail. You have to provide a driver's license number to use a check. There even are cars that have push-button locks whose codes the owners have to memorize.

So far no one has required any special password for public restrooms, but give them time. After all, somebody came up with the idea of pay toilets.

Our computer age has gone beyond just requiring us to memorize enough numerical sequences to keep Albert Einstein confused. Anyone who regularly uses computers has learned they also must have special identities, too.

You can type in your own name, but odds are several hundred other people share your name and you have to pick something else. I feel sorry for anyone named John Smith who tries to create an online ID. Odds are if he types out johnsmith, he'll get a message back saying it has been taken and recommending alternatives, such as johnsmith236842, which means there are 236,841 other John Smiths out there, plus the original johnsmith.

You can get creative by adding to an on-screen identity. For example, John Smith could try johnsmith, only to find there are 287,921 others. Forget jsmith, johns or similar variations, because they've all been taken.

As a result, we've had to come up with alternative identities for ourselves online. People tend to get creative, sometimes creating an ID that reflects something about themselves, such as johnsmithmillionaire (particularly effective for those singles sites) or jsgreasemonkey or johnsmith4u.

Then people start knowing each other by their online identities, and start identifying with their alter egos. Some people create three or four or more online identities, and some of those even have their own separate personalities.

Even Dr. Jeckyll couldn't have imagined having so many Mr. Hydes.

You could get lost out there in the cyber world with so many identities. Not even relocated federally protected witnesses go though so many identity changes.

Actually, it can get difficult trying to keep up with different online identities and making sure you've got the right one for where you are on the information highway. It can be done, although you have to be careful so you don't start sending e-mail from one of your identities to the other.

Well, I guess you could do that, although just as you're all right talking to yourself as long as you don't answer, you'd probably be OK as long as you didn't start a correspondence with yourself.

Naturally, to e-mail yourself or anybody else, you have to get to your mail file, and to do that you have to have a password, and here we are where we started.

"Who lost the 2000 World Series?"

"The Yankees."

Some things never change.

CHAPTER 89
YOU KNOW YOU'VE BEEN
ONLINE TOO LONG WHEN...

L ike many people, I've succumbed to the
wiles of the computer. Once I vowed they'd
take away my typewriter only when they
pried it from my cold, dead fingers. Now, I don't
know what I'd do without the computers in my life.

When it comes to writing and editing, computers have made life so much easier, even though
there are occasions when they move with all the
speed of a glacier moving uphill. Beyond the basic
workaday utilitarian uses of computers and the
many games you can play on them, there is more.
There is the siren call of the Internet.

This is the information highway we used to hear
about. That's a term that's as obsolete as a Texas
Instruments abacus. While you can go on the Net to
research everything from genealogy to learning how
to build an atomic bomb and to send e-mail to family and friends, there's even more.

There's chat. And message boards. And forums.
And clubs. And who-knows-what else for individu-

als to communicate with each other. Just as the Net offers a wide range of research possibilities, it offers an even wider range subjects for folks to talk about with one another.

Actually, the Internet is sort of like a high-tech CB radio, right down to people using "handles" and colorful nicknames, some more colorful than could be mentioned here.

You can electronically discuss Dutch oven recipes, your favorite movie stars, which singers you can't stand, which books you like to read. You can talk about health matters with other people who might have the same malady or advice for treating some ailment. Sports, of course, are big Net topics, too.

There's more.

There are folks talking about more intimate things, discussing topics you wouldn't talk about in front of your mother. Things you wouldn't want your mother to even know you knew about. But, like anything, the Net can become addictive. An e-friend I met online sent me a list of indications that a person might be spending more time online than he or she should. As a public service, I'll share some of them with you.

You know you've been going online too much when:

- A friend stops to check on you because your phone has been busy for a year.
- You placed the refrigerator beside your computer.

- You get a second phone line just to call out for pizza.
- You find out divorce papers were served on you six months ago.
- You talk on the phone with the same person you are sending an instant message to.
- Your teacher or boss recommends a drug test for the blood shot eyes.
- You get up at 2 a.m. to go to the bathroom and turn the computer on instead.
- You start introducing yourself as "Jim @ aol.com."
- All of your friends have an @ in their names.
- You ask the plumber how much it would cost to replace the chair in front of the computer with a toilet.
- Your wife drapes a wig over the monitor to remind you of what she looks like.
- You name your children Explorer, Yahoo and Dotcom.
- You get a tattoo that says, "This body best viewed with Internet Explorer 5.0."
- As your car crashes through the guardrail on a mountain road, your first instinct is to search for the "back" button.
- You forgot how to work the TV remote control.
- You buy a laptop computer and a cell phone so you can chat online in your car.

- You look at an annoying person off line and wish that you had your "ignore" button handy.
- You start to experience withdrawal after not being online for a while.
- You sit on ICQ for six hours waiting for that certain special person to sign on.
- You get up in the morning and go online before getting your coffee.
- You sign off, and your screen says you were on for 3 days and 45 minutes.
- You need to be pried from your computer by the Jaws-of-Life.

CHAPTER 90
HOORAY FOR HOLLYWEIRD
BACK IN THE SADDLE AGAIN

Whatever did happen to Randolph Scott – as the Statler Brothers ask in their song – and all the other Western heroes of yesteryear?

There's been a small amount of hoopla lately over the return of the Western to the movie screen. Some return – two straight Westerns and one spoof. Clint Eastwood is riding the trail again as a mysterious gunslinging stranger, and there's a second Western on the horizon about cowboys fighting a cattle baron.

For those of us who enjoy sagebrush sagas, it's been a long dry spell, and this summer gives us a chance to see something on the silver screen besides blood-crazed maniacs with gardening shears, teenagers with overactive libidos, ghetto residents who have traded tap dancing for break dancing and depressed rich folks trying to deal with being both rich and depressed at the same time.

THOMAS GARRETT

I like movies, all types of movies. In fact, I probably spend most of my time sitting in a theater. But in the last few years, I've really missed the Western. Sure, most of the stories were fairly simple and almost every plot that could be used has been used repeatedly since the first horse opera hit the screen.

It's that simplicity most fans of Westerns seem to like. There's hardly any doubt about who the hero is and who the villain is, or even how the story will end, although Westerns do occasionally have an unexpected twist at the end. You don't have to sit there wondering what's going on, you don't have to try to understand the psychological motivations for why the bad guy is bad and, generally, you don't have to read a half-dozen reviews to decide if its fit to see.

Remember when John Wayne outdid the guys in the black hats time after time, all the way from "Dark Command" to "Rio Lobo"? And when Gary Cooper stood alone against the vengeance-seeking badmen in "High Noon"? How about Alan Ladd's shoot-out with Jack Palance in "Shane," or Henry Fonda's with Walter Brennan's clan in "My Darling Clementine"?

Sure, the old Westerns played a little loose with historical facts, like Charlton Heston playing Buffalo Bill Cody in "Pony Express." Cody was in his teens during the time of the real Pony

Express; Heston wasn't when he played him. But that was all right; audiences could accept some deviation from the facts.

But in the '60s, that era when everything was turned upside down, the Western went downhill. Westerns became political statements, replacing traditional elements with modern-day values. They became grittier, probably a little more realistic and accurate, but they lost their appeal. Nobody wanted to hear a lecture about the evils of modern society disguised as a horse opera. We got all that on the six o'clock news. People wanted to escape those things for a couple of hours and be entertained.

Then there were the spaghetti Westerns, movies made by Italians in a Spanish desert with a cast of French, English and Greek actors, usually with one American thrown in for good measure. Of course, Clint Eastwood made his name in those pasta burners then went on to make regular Westerns for a while.

Movie stars have changed, too, since Westerns slipped from the scene. Instead of handsome actors who could fit into any role, from Westerns to highbrow comedies and drama, we got stars who looked like Cousin Fred and needed psychoanalysis before saying one line.

No matter what critics say, today's actors don't have the range of Wayne, Cooper, Ladd or any other stars who played in Westerns and then could be believable and effective in almost any other type of movie. Clint Eastwood and Charles Bronson are about the only movie actors today versatile enough to start in Westerns.

Can you imagine Al Pacino on horseback? Or Richard Gere in chaps, which would be a challenge since he has a problem just keeping his pants on in most of his movies. How believable could John Travolta be as a sheriff, or Sylvester Stallone as a gunfighter? Could you see Sean Penn as a cow-puncher, or Eddie Murphy as a sheepherder?

If Hollywood – or Hollyweird, considering most of its offerings today – can find somebody who could star in Westerns, then maybe the classic American movie can make a comeback. In this age of science fiction, fantasy, teenage sex comedies and slasher movies, it'd be nice to just sit back, eat popcorn and watch the Old West come alive again on a Saturday afternoon.

Until then, happy trails, partners.

(Subsequently, along came Tom Selleck, Kevin Costner, Robert Duvall, Tommy Lee Jones, Morgan Freeman and a few others who showed they were versatile enough to make Westerns. And thanks to Lonesome Dove *and TNT, TV discovered it could do Westerns well, too.)*

CHAPTER 91
THE CRITTER THAT
ATE CHICAGO

Getting our pants scared off seems to be a favorite American pastime.

I mean, just look at all the money horror movies rake in claw over claw as people shell out their bucks to see the incredibly strange creature that ate Morton Grove. And look at anybody's bestseller list, and you'll find a Stephen King book right there between tomes on how to lose weight and how to make money.

It's been said horrormeister King could make a fortune just publishing his laundry list. Personally, I think right now he could make the bestseller list with just his signature on all his cancelled checks.

Naturally, almost everything King's written has been turned into movies, although most of them are nowhere near the quality of his writing. The other night, Kim and I, along with her mother and aunt, went to see the movie version of one of King's short stories on cheap night at the theater, and I started thinking about the nature of horror flicks.

THOMAS GARRETT

The best ones put basic, everyday normal people into situations with your basic, everyday abnormal people or creatures. In recent horror movies, this has amounted to mainly attractive young people with hyperactive glands being stalked by an unattractive maniac armed with an assortment of kitchen utensils, garden tools and other sharp instruments.

Another basic premise is ecology gone amok, something like a snail of horrendous proportion slithering around eating everything and everyone in sight. One of my favorites is one from the '50s in which giant grasshoppers attack Chicago.

There are some things about horror movies that bother me, besides the blood and gore found in today's variety. What irritates me is the way the allegedly normal people act.

I mean, some of these folks don't catch on to what's happening very fast when everyone around them takes on the appearance of dartboards. I'm talking cases of terminal stupidity here.

For example: They'll go into a creepy, dark house in the middle of the night, knowing there's a deranged killer inside and not bother to turn on the lights. I don't even go into my very uncreepy FHA house at night without turning on the lights.

Not these folks, however. They just wander around, conserving electricity, until something jumps out of a closet and uses them for shish kabob.

Probably the best horror movie line I've heard in this aspect was in the one we saw the other night. In a deserted town where all the adults have been killed, a couple who have found a murdered youth break into a creepy old house, and the woman asks, "Are we safe?"

Everybody in the audience knew the correct answer, but not the couple. Of course, this was before he wound up with a stab wound to the chest, and she was almost sacrificed to a giant gopher.

Then there's the way these folks deal with closed doors. Do they throw them open and stand back to see what's inside? No, they crack them open, stick their heads inside and wind up getting them shoved into a Ronco Veg-a-Matic.

Another real intelligent move these people make is to stay around where they're not wanted. Honestly, would you stay in a house if some strange voice from the kitchen faucet told you to leave? If you drove into a town where there were no people, no cars, no working phones, would you decide this would be a nice place to spend the night?

If your answer is yes to either of these questions, you may have a future as a horror movie victim. A short future.

Oh, well. I guess that's just the nature of the beast. If it weren't for hapless, helpless victims, I guess there wouldn't be any horror movies. After all, who'd be afraid of a monster who didn't have anyone to mash?

CHAPTER 92
ABOUT MICHAEL JACKSON

I'm beginning to wish Michael Jackson would just beat it.

Lately, you can't turn on the television set or check out a magazine cover without seeing him in his Barnum and Bailey uniform, Lone Ranger shades and wethead hairdo. You almost can't change stations on the radio without hearing that high-pitched voice piercing the speaker.

Now, this isn't new with me. I couldn't stand Michael Jackson before puberty hit him – if it ever did – and when he was allegedly crooning with the Jackson Five. I think it had to do with being cooped on a band bus on a long school trip with some clown constantly playing Jackson Five tapes and that even-then high-pitched voice cutting through the air. Several hours of such torture could almost be grounds for justifiable homicide. Or possibly even self-defense.

The real clincher came this week when tickets for Jackson's concert tour with his brothers went on sale. Actually, they're sort of being raffled off at

$30 a pop. Not only wouldn't I pay $30 to see Michael Jackson, I wouldn't pay $30 to see Dolly Parton mud wrestle. (Twenty dollars maybe, but never $30.)

It's expected two million people will shell out $30 a pop to see this twerp. That comes to something like the annual budget of most nations, and doesn't count T-shirt sales, program sales and the sale of assorted souvenirs. With a couple of more tours like that, Michael Jackson could almost wipe out the national debt and still have change.

I'm not sure what brought about this Michael Jackson phenomenon, then again I'm not sure what brings about most phenomenon surrounding performers. I do know he's certainly not that much better of a singer than others in the performing arts. I will admit he's a fair singer for a guy whose voice never changed, but that's all I'll admit about Michael Jackson.

It's been rumored he's really Diana Ross, but I know that's not true. Her voice is lower. The best line I've ever heard from Michael Jackson was at the beginning of his *Thriller* video when he says, "I'm not like other guys."

We're talking understatement here, folks.

Still, he keeps cranking out hit after hit. It probably won't be much longer before Michael Jackson can release a recording of himself yawning and sell a million copies. The video of it probably will do even better.

Those hits also have won him almost every award possible, except in country music circles. And, who knows, he's liable to try hi hand at a country tune just to make a complete sweep.

Of course, it might be interesting to hear Michael Jackson try to sing a Hank Williams Jr. song. And Willie Nelson's sung duets with just about everybody except Michael Jackson and The Monkey Run Boys. So, anything might be possible, although I certainly hope it never occurs. It's an idea that's just not that much of a thriller for me.

(Who knew what a strange trip Michael Jackson would take through the years since I wrote this? It just goes to show that fame can be fleeting, even if people still talk about your antics some 20 years later, although they are talking less. As for the "outrageous" ticket price, $30 is a pretty fair one now, even for a Branson show. And I might even be willing to pay $30 now to see Dolly Parton mud wrestle.)

CHAPTER 93
INQUIRING MINDS WATCH TABLOID TV

I've got to get this off my chest, as difficult as it may be for me to make this confession. Every now and then, I like to watch Geraldo Rivera.

And I've been sneaking a peek at Sally Jesse Raphael and, occasionally, I've checked in on Oprah, most recently her celebrated how-she-took-it-off show. I've never seen Morton Downey Jr., but I'm not sure I'd want to. Even I have my standards.

Many in my business would be aghast at learning of my guilty pleasures since tabloid tube bashing is the current fad among "serious" journalists. Other than conducting research, those folks would never watch such programs because they're beneath their lofty standards. Or, at least, they'd never admit tuning in Geraldo just for the heck of it and to see what he's up to now.

These are the same people who would never be caught expanding their inquiring minds at the supermarket checkout stands, although they might glance at the headlines. While I agree the taste of programs such as Geraldo's and others isn't always the best, you've got to admit they're never dull.

Where else can you see a gay, right-wing, minority witchcraft practitioner just back from a trip aboard a UFO debate the merits of holistic dentistry with Shirley MacLaine?

"The MacNeil/Lehrer Report" and "Wall street Week" might be more informative, uplifting and tasteful, but when was the last time you saw Louis Rukeyser get into a brawl with a stocks analyst? Or William F. Buckley Jr. call one of his guests a piece of scum, at least in terms most of us could understand?

I guess it's just morbid curiosity that prompts me to occasionally watch one of the tabloid shows That, and the fact there may be nothing else on at the moment to watch. Most of the time, I'll just move on through the channels unless it really grabs my attention.

Seeing chairs being thrown into the audience, or an 800-pound individual being interviewed, or just hearing certain phrases are among some of the attention grabbers that have caused me to pause and watch. True, they are loaded with sensationalism and sometimes deliberately tug at sentimental threads in our psyches, and they may be the journalistic equivalent of professional wrestling, but these shows do serve a purpose. At the least, they entertain us at our basest levels, but they also can prompt us to try and be a little more aware of what's happening in society.

While some folks think these shows may be harmful, I don't fully agree. They may provide a forum for some blithering idiot to espouse a repulsive cause like Nazism or an equally disgusting philosophy. But they also give viewers a chance to see just what these individuals are like and expose them for the knot heads they really are. I mean, once you see and listen to some of these folks, how can a sensible person put any store in their message.

Still, there are those shows about female mud wrestling and Chippendale dancers in between such philosophical, and sometimes pugilistic, discussion. But, after all, even tabloid TV can't survive on serious issues alone.

(This was pre-Jerry Springer, who brought tabloid TV to a whole new level with gay midget transsexual food wrestling.)

CHAPTER 94
A WORD FROM OUR SPONSOR

"**D**o you know what the dentist told us today? Our teeth aren't getting clean enough!"

"Are you suffering from the heartbreak of psoriasis?"

"She's a beautiful girl, but she has dandruff. What a turn-off!"

"Nothing personal, but I think you really should try my mouthwash."

"Oh, these ugly brown spots!"

How often have you heard these and similar phrases? To hear the Madison Avenue types tell it, we're a nation of untouchables who should ring brass bells and shout "Unclean" as we walk along. Unless, of course, we happen to use the products they push, which are guaranteed to make each and every one of us socially acceptable.

Yes, friends, we've got trouble with a capital T, and that rhymes with C, and that stands for Commercial.

According to commercials, our breath stinks, we

suffer a variety of skin ailments and our toilet bowls are perpetually dull.

Commercials tell us we use the wrong laundry detergent, can't see ourselves in our dishes, and our neighbors run away screaming in terror because our underarm deodorant isn't powerful enough.

Commercials make people think we're a nation afflicted with halitosis, indigestion and terminal ring-around-the-collar and whose children are ashamed to be seen in public because our toilet paper isn't soft.

Commercials leave the impression our pets are likely to rip our throats out at any second because we haven't been feeding them food with the taste they enjoy. How do advertising executives know how delicious dog food is? And did you ever wonder if your pet really cares that its food comes in shapes to match the flavor?

Of course, the worst of the lot are those commercials that fill the airwaves on cable television. They also can be found on regular stations in the afternoons and after 10 at night. You know the ones I'm talking about, like the one that offers us every recording ever made by Max Schnickel, the world's greatest yodeling piano tuner and Number One recording artist in the Ukraine.

I like the ones for the assorted tools and utensils, like the Wonder Wheel.

Announcer: "Yes, it's the wondrous Wonder Wheel! It slices, dices, chops, hops, bops and makes fantastic cole slaw. But wait, that's not all! If you order before 3 this afternoon, you get the Knick Knack Knife with the reinforced stainless tin foil blade which cuts meat so thin you only have to buy one roast a year and can be used to trim cedar trees.

"But there's more! For a limited time only, you also will receive Fabulous Flab Fighter. Yes, friends, with this super-strong rubber band attached to any door knob you can exercise just like the actors getting paid a ridiculous sum for looking stupid in this commercial.

"How much would you expect to pay for this marvelous merchandise? $99.95? $59.95? No! For this time only, you can get all these goodies for the low price of $9.95, plus $1,232.53 in postage and handling."

Oh, what hard times we lie in today. If we don't use the correct toothpaste, bathe with the right soap and gargle with the proper mouthwash, we run the risk of becoming social outcasts. We absolutely can't live without these fantastic new devices that can only be purchased through television offers.

Sometimes I wonder how our forebears survived without deodorant soap, hair spray and toilet bowl cleaner. And at other times, I wonder if we'll survive deodorant soap, hair spray and toilet bowl cleaner.

If Madison Avenue has its way, we won't be able to survive without their products.

And now, a word from our sponsor.

(To these annoying commercials you now can add today's spots for hair-growth products, herpes treatments and "ED".)

CHAPTER 95
EVEN WITHOUT HORSES, IT CAN BE A WESTERN

I dozed off in the recliner watching a movie the other night, which really isn't that unusual.

Anyway, the movie was about a stranger who rides into a dying little town whose population is under the thumb of a vicious gang. The stranger (which also happens to be the name of the movie) is out for revenge against the gang's leader and in short order starts dispatching them until the final showdown.

This sounds pretty much like a typical kind of Western, sort of like Clint Eastwood's *High Plains Drifter*. Except, instead of horses the stranger and gang were riding Harleys, and Kathy Long, a former world kickboxing champion, was playing Clint Eastwood.

I've been noticing that some movies in the last few years really are Westerns, they just don't have horses and Stetsons. One of my guilty pleasures is *Road House*, which TBS and TNT play about once a month. It has Western written all over it.

Instead of being a gunslinger, Patrick Swayze is a bouncer whose reputation precedes him. He gets crossways with Ben Gazarra, the bad guy who runs roughshod over the town where Swayze comes to cleanup a bar. There's plenty of action as Swayze confronts Gazarra's thugs in various showdowns before they ultimately square off against one another.

While honest-to-goodness Westerns may be in short supply (except for Tom Selleck and TNT's efforts), Western story lines sure keep getting tapped by screenwriters. Maybe it's because Westerns traditionally are fairly clear-cut stories.

You have the good guys, the bad guys and the background characters there to give them something to fight about. Good guy rides into town, finds himself drawn to affable townspeople, ticks off the local bad guy and his gang, and it all comes down to a final showdown. In the end, the good guy either settles down with one of the affable women of the town or rides off into the sunset in search of more affable townspeople to defend.

That plot worked in numerous movies for John Wayne, Audie Murphy, James Stewart, Randolph Scott, Gary Cooper, Alan Ladd, Clint Eastwood and even Tom Selleck as well as an untold number of other Western stars.

Actually, a Western is more a feeling than a setting. There even have been Westerns that are set in outer space. John Carpenter had a Western set on Mars. (One of his first movies actually was a Western set in besieged police precinct house.) Sean Connery even starred in a sci fi version of *High Noon* a few years ago.

Just because a movie has a contemporary or futuristic setting doesn't mean it's not a Western. If you could replace the cars or spaceships with horses, then it could be a Western.

But while I might doze off while watching a female kickboxer clean up a town, I won't be falling asleep when *The Magnificent Seven* is on. Now, there's an idea for a movie. A small planet being threatened by an intergalactic gang hires seven laser blaster slingers ...

Thought for the Week: "Don't ever squat when wearing spurs."

CHAPTER 96
THE ELVIS TRILOGY

(These next three columns were written at different times, but they just go so well together,)

CHAPTER 97
ST. ELVIS?

There was a special on a cable channel the other night about Elvis Presley fans. And since fan is short for fanatic, the term definitely fits these somewhat strange folks.

For example, there was a woman whose husband left her because her adoration for Elvis crossed the threshold from rational to looney tune time. The same woman's daughter once got to be on stage with Elvis. When she died afterwards, she was buried in the same dress she wore on that occasion, along with a recording of "Burning Love." To be honest, this woman looked like a holdover from the Geraldo Rivera drug special the night before.

Then there were the twin sisters who believed Elvis was their father. The sisters said their mother never told them Elvis was their father, but that mom never told them he wasn't their father, either. I'm not sure how the two sisters planned to work it out, but they had planned to name their firstborn child Elvis Aaron Presley Jr. However, they couldn't wait so they gave that name to their dog, then decided their first-born would be Elvis Aaron Presley III.

And there were others.

One guy, who looked as if he hadn't bathed since Elvis died, changed his name to Elvis Presley because his friends said he looked like the singer. Actually, the fellow looked like Goober Lindsay in a Harpo Marx fright wig.

Another individual was an Elvis impersonator who, because of his girth, must have specialized in the singer's latter years. His son also had a little Elvis suit and slicked back hair. The boy looked embarrassed by the whole affair.

I'm still not sure if this was a spoof of documentaries, or if these were real people. If they were real, then I'd say these folks were in dire need of psychological counseling as soon as possible, and they should not be allowed to handle sharp instruments.

Now, there are certain entertainers I'm fond of, and I try to watch them at the movies or on television whenever possible. There are singers and musicians I like and enjoy seeing in concert if I can make it. And I think that's the way most folks are.

But some, and the majority seem to be Elvis fans, apparently have popped a clutch somewhere. They seem to think Elvis, even a dead Elvis, can work miracles and, at the very least, want to see him become a saint.

Folks, we're talking about a singer here, an exceedingly popular singer, true. This was a guy from

Tupelo who had the good fortune to have an excellent singing voice and happened to come along at the right time in the right place. And that's great. But Elvis never could walk across the Mississippi without a bridge.

And it was fan like those in that show the other night who helped make him a prisoner of his own success behind the walls of Graceland. From all accounts, he probably would have been happier if he'd kept on driving a truck. I like Elvis, and still enjoy listening to his music, but all the folks dancing on his grave to make a buck have made him a tired act in my book.

Years after he keeled over in his bathroom, Elvis still is making money for folks who make grave robbers seem respectable. There are folks out there selling everything from splinters from the basement door at Graceland to tiny vials of alleged Elvis sweat.

There are Elvis bottles, books, balloons and bumper stickers; Elvis pens, pins, pencils, pictures and posters; Elvis cassettes, cars, capes, caps, cakes and cookies.

I tried to change the channel the other night, but the folks in the documentary were so unreal it fascinated me, and I couldn't bring myself to do it. Watching those poor, demented souls being exploited as much as Elvis has been left me feeling as disgusted with myself for watching them as I was with the documentary's makers.

So, I decided to throw in my two cents' worth

with this column in order to say this. Elvis has been dead for years, it's time everyone let him rest in peace and stopped filling the pockets of these ghouls.

That would be the best tribute his fans could give him.

CHAPTER 98
ELVIS LIVES?

If you happen to believe the grocery store tabloids, folks in Kalamazoo may have a king living in their midst. Yes, friends, some say Elvis lives and has chosen to make the Michigan city his new home.

Actually, the "Elvis lives" rumors even sparked that hot shot of television journalists, Geraldo Rivera, into doing a special report for that bastion of TV journalism, "Entertainment Tonight." Of course, it's only natural for Geraldo to check into it since he had a weeklong series of reports last year about women who claimed Elvis fathered their children and young ladies who claimed they bore more than a passing resemblance to the singer.

According to the latest rumors, Elvis decided he needed some privacy and a normal life. After all, Elvis lived in a public fish bowl anytime he ventured beyond the Graceland gates at Memphis. So, he faked his death in a bathroom at the mansion and slipped away in the midst of the anguish and confusion of his fans at his alleged passing.

Eventually, so the story goes, Elvis ended up at Kalamazoo, where he's gone bald, grown a beard and spends a lot of time hanging around a Burger King.

A television station there is running commercials saying Elvis just liked the station's programming so much he decided to settle at Kalamazoo. And another TV station in Hollyweird, following the time-honored traditions and high standards of broadcast journalism, has spent the ratings sweep running a series investigating the question of "Does Elvis Live?" A rival station is running the promotion "Elvis is still dead" and its newscasts deal with more pressing matters.

I'm afraid I have to agree: Elvis is as dead as a doornail. In fact, Elvis is as dead as Francisco Franco, and that's about as dead as you can get. No matter what some woman at a Kalamazoo burger joint thinks, or some fan whose elevator doesn't reach the top floor believes, poor ol' Elvis has left the planet.

Of course, it does help sell grocery store tabloids and gives Geraldo something to do when he's not unsealing empty vaults and visiting Charles Manson. The "Elvis lives" stories are on the same level as World War II bombers on the moon, abominable snowmen kidnapping Nepalese women as mates and 115-year-old Yugoslavians fathering children.

I think the ultimate story would be learning that abominable aliens took Elvis away aboard a UFO to teach him the universe's secrets for weight loss.

These are great fantasies and can be a relief from the real world news, as long as folks realize the difference, Somehow, an abominable snowman isn't quite as frightening as an abominable Panamanian strongman. And, to me at least, folks saying Elvis lives aren't quite as sleazy as folks saying Elvis was their secret lover and father of their children, and you can learn all about it for $19.95.

Someday, the one-time truck driver from Tupelo who just wanted to make a record for his mama may rest in peace. Until then, I guess he'll have to put up with the rumors, wherever he may be.

CHAPTER 99
GRANDPA ELVIS

I wonder what the tabloids are going to do now that Elvis' only acknowledged daughter is about to become a mother. That would make Elvis, had he survived, a grandfather.

And don't you imagine that the idea of Grandpa Elvis is adding a few gray airs to the heads of fans everywhere?

Yes, little Lisa Marie, who only got married a couple of weeks ago, is, as they used to say, about a month along in the family way. Gee, with all these women claiming to have been Elvis' lovers and having had illegitimate children by him, it's ironic that he almost had an illegitimate grandchild.

I bet the Enquirer, the Globe and Bird Cage Liner Weekly all are scrambling to get exclusive stories and pictures. Of course, I will fearlessly predict that in about eight months we'll be swamped with stories of a mystery man with a pompadour and sideburns being seen outside the nursery at whatever hospital the tyke is born. And I'll give you three guesses who they'll say the mystery man is,

393

and it won't be John Lennon, either.

What a field day the tabs can have.

"Grandpa Elvis Slips Into Hospital to See Grandchild!"

"Nurse: I Knew He Wasn't Dead!"

"I Sold Pampers to Elvis!!"

"Boy Trapped in Refrigerator, Eats Own Foot!!!"

(I know the last one doesn't have anything to do with Elvis, but it's my favorite tabloid headline.)

Yes, there'll be more Elvis sightings next year than Carter has little liver pills. Then Geraldo and Sally Jesse and Oprah will have interviews with people who claim to have met The King on his way to visit his grandchild.

"That's right, Geraldo, this guy just gave me the keys to a Cadillac and just asked that I make sure his grandbaby gets a regular supply of formula."

"Why, I couldn't believe it was him, but he showed me his rhinestones and cape and curled his lip, and I knew it was Elvis."

"I told Martha that no matter what Elvis ain't left Graceland since '77, but I was wrong. There he was bigger than life. Shoot, he hadn't lost a bit of weight since he died, and he still looked better than my brother-in-law."

"What was strange is that he said that statue on Mars wasn't of him, but that it's really a memorial to Liberace."

Of course, all these stories and interviews will be about as reliable as a screen door on a submarine

– there'll just be too many holes in them. But folks will snatch up those checkout-stand gazettes so fast you'll think they're giving them away.

Yes, I know this isn't particularly respectful to Elvis' memory, but it's in fun. Those other folks try to make their readers think their stories are true. Unfortunately, there are indeed people who sincerely believe there's a statue of Elvis on Mars, and that he's wolfing down Whoppers at some Midwestern Burger King.

Personally, I hope Elvis' daughter can have her baby in peace and not have to deal too much with those ink-stained vultures who pass themselves off as journalists. Peace, Lisa Marie, and good luck.

And peace to you, too, Elvis, wherever you are.

(In 1989, Lisa Marie Presley gave birth to a baby girl, Danielle.)

CHAPTER 100
FAMILY & SPECIAL PEOPLE
HOW WE SPENT OUR
SUMMER VACATIONS

I've always liked vacations. Of course, I suppose most people like vacations, except those workaholic types who haven't figured out how to work in their sleep, so they can enjoy laboring 24/7.

Even when having to pick huckleberries at the crack of dawn, I've enjoyed going on vacation. I enjoy it more than working, although work does have its advantages, such as the paycheck that keeps various creditors and utilities happy.

Vacations always have been good times. When I was a youngster, I almost always got a fresh haircut and a new comic book or two before we left on vacation. That was when comics cost 12 cents and haircuts were about one or two bucks.

With my cowlick sticking up and my new comic book atop a stack of old ones, I'd sit in the back seat and bury my nose in various superhero adventures while Dad pointed the car down the road, and Mom told him how to get where we were going. After a while, I'd take in the scenery and wonder if we were there yet.

It seemed to take a lot longer to get places then, even though the speed limit was much higher than now. Now, everything seems to go much faster. Especially vacations.

From my back seat vantage point, I'd watch the countryside fly past and wonder what was growing in that field, how deep is this river (and isn't there another bridge besides this narrow one) and who would live in that rickety old shack?

This was when there were still "See Rock City" billboards around. I always wondered where Rock City was and why you should see it.

If we weren't visiting my Aunt Dorothy, going on vacation meant we got to stay in motels. I always liked that, and I think Eli and Amelia inherited it from me because they like to stay at motels, too.

These weren't expensive motels, by any means. Many looked like those motor courts in *Bonnie and Clyde*, with little separated cottages, a circle drive and a couple of trees or shrubs out front. Usually there was a neon sign with a red flashing arrow pointing toward the office.

In the room, I usually wound up getting the bed at the back of the room. You could sit on the bed, watch TV and eat snacks, things you didn't do at home. I even got to stay up to watch the late movie when we were on vacation. Generally, the air conditioner was in the window above or beside my bed, and motel blankets were notoriously thin.

After we ate supper, Dad would sit out in front of our cottage or room, usually in one of those round-backed metal patio chairs, and visit with other guests. Or he'd go down to the motel office that almost always had a coffee pot on and visit with the desk clerk and everybody else who stopped in there. Dad never met a stranger.

At least he'd do that when he wasn't checking the oil or transmission fluid or something else on the car. Ours were the original driving vacations. We spent much of the time on the road, driving from place to place, stopping occasionally to see some site or other, then hitting the road again. Because of that, Dad insisted the car had to be in tip-top condition.

Plus, as a mechanic, he just liked to tinker with it, too.

Those were fun times. Just getting away from home for a few days and seeing other places was fun. That's what vacations are for anyway.

So, if you haven't had a vacation this year, hurry up and take one. Do something you enjoy, do something your family enjoys, make some memories.

CHAPTER 101
GUMBALLS, SUNDAY DINNER AND AUNT MAGGIE

A unt Maggie always had grape bubble gum in her purse at church.

She carried it so us heathens would behave ourselves during the sermon. Whenever I went to church with Uncle Grady, Aunt Maggie and my cousins, I could always count on getting a piece of grape bubble gum.

It was the kind that looked like jawbreakers, big, round purple globes of gum. It was always sweet, and the grape flavor lasted a long time, longer than it does nowadays.

Sometimes she had the red gum balls, and those were hot. It was cinnamon, and it definitely got your attention.

Whenever I see the boxes on store shelves filled with gumballs I think about Aunt Maggie and how she handed them out to us youngsters.

I liked being around Aunt Maggie. When I was about 5 or 6, I stayed with her and Uncle Grady and my cousins -- Bernice, Dean and Roy Lee -- while my Dad and Mom were with my grandpa during his last days. They lived in the country on a dusty East Texas road. Most country roads in East Texas were dusty then because rocks were scarce.

I learned to eat pinto beans at Aunt Maggie's table. She didn't fix them any differently than Mom did, but somehow -- at the time -- hers just seemed better. It might have had something to do with the way she let Dean and Roy Lee fix their beans on their plates. They mashed them up and sprinkled them with black pepper, so being the younger cousin, I naturally followed their example.

Aunt Maggie always had something good to eat at her kitchen table. Kim still fixes a recipe for Creole Cabbage that she got from Aunt Maggie. And through most of my memory, she had the same kitchen table, a heavy wooden table with rounded corners and edges, darkened with age and the occasional cigarette burn from where Uncle Grady had let his Camel sit too long.

Even after I got older, and they moved into town, it seemed I always found Aunt Maggie in the kitchen. She was either cooking or canning or just sitting at the table with a cup of coffee and a cigarette burning away in an ancient wooden ashtray.

She always had a battered old tin dipper hanging from the cabinet by the sink, a carryover from the days when water was dipped from a bucket.

Even after Bernice, Dean and Roy Lee had married and moved on to their own lives and families, Aunt Maggie fixed dinner every Sunday for her brood. Whether they made it home or not, she had it ready for them every Sunday.

Although we alternated the location of the family reunion we used to have every August, eventually it wound up with a permanent location at Aunt Maggie and Uncle Grady's house. When all the brothers, sisters, children, grandchildren and, ultimately, great-grandchildren showed up, the neighbors thought it was an invasion.

That, too, was usually on a Sunday, a sort of daylong dinner on the ground.

Aunt Maggie loved her little 'uns, no matter how big they got. Plenty of photos hung from her walls and sat in frames on tables, shelves and on top of the TV set. And almost any youngster could qualify as one of her little 'uns. How she loved children.

Things were tough for her for a while after Uncle Grady died 20 years ago. He'd been sick a long time. She stayed beside him the whole time, taking care of him. She made adjustments as people do after losing their life's partner and got along all right, but she never stopped missing him.

Many years ago, we thought we were going to lose Aunt Maggie. In fact, the doctors had told the family to be prepared. But something happened. She told us afterward that she'd seen a great golden city, and in the city there was a man who had his back to her. He wouldn't turn around for some reason, and she was convinced he was Uncle Grady, and it wasn't her time to go.

She got better after that, although she never fully recovered her health. Aunt Maggie got along pretty good for a while, but slowly the years caught up with her.

She went to the hospital last weekend. Then, on Tuesday, Aunt Maggie went home with Uncle Grady.

I hope the cherubs like grape bubble gum.

CHAPTER 102
A TRUE FISH STORY

Let's hope we get through this Friday without another storm. After two in a row, it almost could make one dread the approach of Friday, a day usually greeted with cheers instead of fear.

We were out of town and managed to miss last Friday's big blow. We've managed to get caught up on the stories about the storm, but the most interesting came from Mary Wolverton.

Mrs. Wolverton, whom I met at a craft show, called here at Sixth and Hickory earlier this week about a personal tragedy that resulted from the storm. George didn't survive it.

George, by the way, was an 18-inch long fantail goldfish. A goldfish who apparently could predict approaching storms, tornados in particular.

It seems Mrs. Wolverton and her husband also were out of town when the storm struck. Their neighbors called them Saturday about the storm and the power outage that accompanied it.

The power outage appears to have been

THOMAS GARRETT

George's downfall, according to Mrs. Wolverton. When the power went out, the pump on George's tank ceased functioning. Eventually, so did George, whom Mrs. Wolverton found floating in his tank.

For some reason, she said, it didn't affect George's tank mate, Henry, a 10-inch goldfish. Mrs. Wolverton noted that goldfish, being related to the carp, is a hardier fish than some people would believe.

Mrs. Wolverton said they'd had George five years, and he'd moved here with them from Missouri. She met George at a medical office. Mrs. Wolverton said whenever she'd go in for an appointment, this one particular goldfish in a tank at the doctor's office would have a fit and splash about, even splashing her. She mentioned the fish's reaction to her to its owner, and he offered to let her have it.

So, George moved in with the Wolvertons.

George was a rather large goldfish and couldn't eat just plain goldfish food. Mrs. Wolverton said be required a special, larger fish food about the size of a pea. It wasn't stocked locally since there wasn't much demand for it here, so she had to get George's food in Springfield. His appetite wasn't limited to his special food, Mrs. Wolverton added.

Many fish are known to eat smaller fish or other aquatic life that is introduced into their tanks. Mrs. Wolverton said George had a taste for the tiny snails people use to help keep their fish tanks clean. She said whenever she'd put the snails into

George's tank, she soon would find only their shells.

Now, about George's meteorological capabilities.

Mrs. Wolverton said George could predict approaching tornadoes. She first noticed when last November's tornado tore through the area. Before the tornado struck, Mrs. Wolverton said she noticed George's unusual activity. She said he started flopping around in his tank and splashing water and just having a fit.

Shortly after that, the storm moved through the area. Mrs. Wolverton said she began observing George, and that he acted the same way whenever there was a tornado or severe storms in the area.

Apparently, George had better luck at predicting bad weather than some human forecasters.

I listened to Mrs. Wolverton's story about George and was intrigued by it enough to share it with you. Please don't think I'm making light of either Mrs. Wolverton or George.

Folks have known for years that changes in the atmosphere before a storm can cause unusual reactions by animals, and many have watched animals to determine what the weather will be. Scientists even are studying animal reactions to determine if they're able to sense impending earthquakes. So, I have great respect for the animal kingdom's uncanny abilities in that area.

I'm also sure Mrs. Wolverton will miss George, his antics and his weather-predicting abilities. I certainly hope George is happy in that great fish tank in the beyond, and that he has food and snails in abundance.

CHAPTER 103
EVEN NOW, UNCLE BEN
ALWAYS WILL BE THERE

Uncle Ben always was there whenever any-one needed him. Whether it was a family crisis or just somebody needing a hand, he was more than willing to help. I remember any time anyone in our family was sick or in the hospital, Uncle Ben checked on them and was ready to do whatever needed doing. When there were deaths in the family, he always seemed to be the steady one, I guess what they call theses days as the "go-to guy."

Uncle Ben was married to my Mom's sister, Johnnie. It was easy to get tongue-tied and refer to them as Uncle Ben and Uncle Johnnie. He was her second husband. Aunt Johnnie's first husband was killed in World War II.

Uncle Ben was a World War II veteran, too. He was in the engineers and helped build airfields throughout the South Pacific. I remember seeing some of his pictures from the war, those small snap-shots that so many veterans brought home. He had pictures of the grader he operated, some showing him pushing away earth to level the ground for runways.

Others showed him and his buddies out in the boonies of some jungle island, and there were photos of other construction equipment and military hardware. There were even some shots of South Seas islanders who lived on some of those islands. While I remember one or two "National Geographic shots," these women weren't the South Seas beauties of the movies.

After the war, Uncle Ben stayed in the construction business as a grader operator, or a maintainer operator as they were called then. He traveled around Texas and other parts of the country and helped build anything that needed earth moved. Interstate highways, paper mills, power plants, every kind of road project, you name it, and he helped lay the foundation for it.

Uncle Ben was one of the best grader operators around. No matter how shallow or deep a cut needed to be made, he could set his blade right on the mark, no more and no less.

In my earliest memories of Uncle Ben, he and Aunt Johnnie lived at Irving, between Dallas and Fort Worth, and traveled around Texas, Oklahoma and Louisiana before they finally settled in northeast Texas. A couple of times, Uncle Ben stayed with us when he was working on a project. He'd be out before sunrise and back home after dark.

Depending on the job, that could be his routine seven days a week. Uncle Ben always had a "farmer's tan," his face, arms and hands a deep brown from working all day in the sun. It gave him a rugged look. For work, Uncle Ben usually wore khakis. That was before khakis became casual wear. When he wasn't working, Uncle Ben liked to dress well. Not fancy, but nice, usually a Western shirt and slacks, cowboy boots and a hat. He wore the Stetsons like the ones worn by Harry Truman and LBJ, a felt one for winter and a straw one for summer.

Uncle Ben also enjoyed a good meal. He was a steak eater who could eat steak at almost every meal. In fact, he was a meat-and-potatoes man. That's what he ate almost every day of his life, often fried. He probably would have been a dietitian's nightmare. And until a few years ago he always smoked Kools, too. Even at that, he turned 90 in August.

We hadn't thought of that as being his last birthday. As I said, Uncle Ben always was there. Until last Saturday night.

Of course, he's just not there physically now. I'm sure, in one way or another, Uncle Ben always will be there, at least in our memories.

CHAPTER 104
RECALLING FOND MEMORIES OF MAMA LUCY

No one should have to bury their mama on Mother's Day.

Unfortunately, that's what Kim's mother, Jo, and her sisters, Jane and Joy, had to do for their mother, Lucy Harmon. Mama Lucy, as folks knew her, and she knew lots of folks in her 82 years. Almost anywhere you went in the town of Mayfield, Ky., you'd find somebody who knew Mama Lucy.

Mama Lucy was one of those rare persons who seemed bigger than life. She was a big woman, in height, and her presence could dominate a room. It was hard to miss this tall, big-voiced Kentucky belle who never met a stranger. She reminded me of another Lucy -- a tall, silver-haired Lucille Ball. Mama Lucy carried herself the same way, even dressing somewhat like the beloved comedienne and creating that same kind of presence everywhere she went.

Anytime you met her, you almost always heard her say, "Come over here and give Mama

Lucy a hug." Or, "Well, what'd you bring me?"

Kim told me about her grandmother before I first met Mama Lucy, and she sounded like a wonder woman. She was. For years, Mama Lucy worked as a chef -- not a cook, a chef -- for the Kentucky State Parks. She ran the kitchen at Barkley Lodge, the state-owned resort on Kentucky Lake, where she oversaw no telling how many banquets, brunches, breakfasts, buffets, state functions, receptions, parties and plain old get-togethers. There seemed to be few things Mama Lucy couldn't prepare. She seemed particularly fond of finger foods and appetizers, and her rolls were the finest to ever melt butter.

Over the years, Mama Lucy prepared meals for governors, movie stars, singers and untold bigwigs, concocting fancy dishes and elaborate spreads. Her work even earned her recognition as a Kentucky Colonel. When it came to food service and management, Mama Lucy was the manager's manager.

Even in retirement, she looked at everything in any restaurant or cafe where she went with a critical eye. Mama Lucy seemed to know everybody in the food business around Mayfield, from the owners to the waitresses to the cooks to the busboys and dishwashers, from Majestic's to K&N Drive-In to Hardee's.

It wasn't unusual for her to offer suggestions or advice to those at places she frequented regularly. In a bedroom at her house there hung a small plaque and a framed letter from the owner of a business honoring Mama Lucy for her help in turning its food service around and making it a success. He praised her for volunteering her time to make it work

Mama Lucy also cooked for neighbors, friends and family. She always insisted you eat whenever you went to her house. Hardly a dinner at her church or a potluck supper at the senior center went by without at least one dish from Mama Lucy. Seeing people bringing food to her house before her funeral just seemed a bit ironic to me.

She liked working at the senior center, helping the folks there and fixing food for them. She liked working anywhere and being around people. I think giving away her time kept Mama Lucy young a lot longer. I was surprised at how many younger people, from places she frequented and her church, stopped by for visitation and her services. In a way, it seemed odd that so many had been touched by Mama Lucy.

But that's the way she was. Most of the time Mama Lucy was cheerful and vibrant, and it could be contagious. Sure, she had her darker moments like all of us, and there were occasions when she could be a pain in the rear, but overall those were rare. Mama Lucy was a jubilant spirit, in love with life and all it had to offer.

She saw the world change a lot since she entered it in 1917, witnessing the advent, and demise, of so much through the years. It's still a little hard to believe it's only been a week since Mama Lucy left this world. There had been a few years of health problems that slowed her down somewhat, but she kept going until she just couldn't go any more. The timing may not have been the best, but contrary to the old saying I don't think any day's a particularly good day to die, and some are worse than others.

But that's not something for us to decide. In Mama Lucy's case, maybe those who knew her could agree that perhaps the Good Lord just wanted a good, home-cooked meal from the best chef in Kentucky.

CHAPTER 105
OF CAMARADERIE, FATHERS, SONS AND WORMDROWNERS

By now, Jim Mobley's already started making plans for next year's gathering of the Wormdrowners, a scant week after this group of hardy souls spent their 25th convocation hunting trout.

I first met Jim a couple of months ago when he stopped by the office here at Sixth and Hickory with an invitation to come eat steak with the Wormdrowners. Now, I've never been one to turn down a steak dinner, so I had no problem putting one on my calendar two months in advance.

To be honest, I wasn't too sure what to expect from these guys when I pulled in at Peal's Resort last week. Every year the Wormdrowners have come here, they've stayed at Peal's. It's part of their tradition, as is the pre-fishing day steak dinner with all the trimmings and an assortment of beverages.

It took about, oh, three seconds to feel at ease. Jim reminds you of a favorite uncle, the one who always used to let you get away with stuff when your folks weren't around. He and Baldwin and the others quickly made me feel at home. After spending most of the week covering court, that was great. Add to it a pleasant spring evening with a nice sunset and you could ask for little more.

As I mentioned, this was the 25th annual Wormdrowners' trout hunt. Jim explained the history of this gathering. It started with a group of men from the Midwest who worked in the food service industry, most of them for ARA. This was a high-pressure time for them when they had to put together projections and other reports for the coming year, according to Jim, who retired to Mountain Home.

They started taking fishing trips here to relieve the pressure. Jim said they'd have a dinner, unwind, and then go trout fishing out at Rose's Trout Dock. Like Peal's Resort, they've always used Rose's. After a day of fishing, they gather for another dinner and hand out a few awards -- some genuine, some gag. After enjoying another evening of friendship, they head back to their jobs.

Over the years, the group has changed and grown. Five original Wormdrowners made this year's trip. Others have joined, and it has even become a generational tradition with some of the men's sons now participating as full-blown Wormdrowners. Two of Jim's sons, Keith and Bert, were there last Thursday night. Wormdrowners came from Missouri, Illinois, Kansas, Indiana, Tennessee, Texas and Oklahoma.

In fact, Keith set up a Web page for his pop, who discovered the joys of the Internet, so he could pass along Wormdrowner information an e-mail fellow Wormdrowners and family members.

There were about two dozen or so Wormdrowners in attendance this year. Gathered at wooden picnic tables underneath a pavilion, the aroma of thick, sizzling steaks in the air, they shared stories of past trips and poked good-humored fun at one another. I can't really pass some of the stories along here, at least not without changing identities to protect the guilty.

Jim was the brunt of a good portion of the ribbing, but with an impish grin he dished it out as well as he took it. He made sure everybody had plenty to eat and drink. He's the organizer, the co-ordinator, and the heart of the Wormdrowners. Bert said his dad starts getting ready for the next gathering as soon as the current one's finished.

What impressed me about the Wormdrowners was their sense of camaraderie. Even though some have gone their separate ways, they still return for their annual fishing trip.

But it's not so much for the fishing as it is for seeing each other again, sharing a few laughs, some memories and enjoying one another's company in the heart of the Ozarks.

Something else that struck me was the camaraderie between Jim and his sons. Keith and Bert spoke glowingly of their dad with undisguised pride for him, just as Jim spoke highly of them.

419

They're two of five siblings who grew up moving around the country as their dad's job took them from place to place. Jim said they were gypsies.

That probably helped make them closer, more appreciative of each other, said Keith.

Such feelings seem rare these days, both between fathers and sons and among any group of people.

After getting to meet the Wormdrowners -- and even getting a Wormdrowner T-shirt -- I'm impressed with them. Maybe next year I might get a chance to fish with them. If they fish as well as they tell stories, it could be an interesting experience.

CHAPTER 106
A MAN WHO ENJOYED
A GOOD LAUGH

Jim Ball liked a good joke. Shoot, he even seemed to like bad jokes. He laughed at a few of mine, and they don't get much worse than that.

During the past several years, there have only been a few weekdays when I didn't see Mountain Home's fire chief. Oh, it might have just been a greeting in passing, or an exchange of waved when driving down the street. But, more often than not, generally we'd run into each other at the lounge shared by the city's firemen and policemen.

Altogether over the years, a lot of time has been spent sitting in those old vinyl-covered chairs in the lounge, drinking coffee and sharing stories. Many a tale, tall and otherwise, has been told there. If Jim wasn't the one telling a story, you could bet he'd be the one laughing the hardest. He must have enjoyed laughing because he could laugh so quickly and freely.

And it wasn't a snicker or a giggle, but a full-fledged, hearty roar of laughter that I'll always remember.

Jim took pleasure in practical jokes and gags as well. Often, he would be in the midst of the conspirators, laying the groundwork to snare the unsuspecting target of the gag. They weren't cruel or vicious practical jokes, although you might not want to repeat them in a more genteel surrounding than a company of men.

Sometimes, I'd find myself caught in the middle of a gag, following Jim down the path I knew would lead me to being the butt of the punch line. I didn't mind because usually I'd wait for the next victim to come along and, as a spectator then, watch Jim help lead the next poor soul into the joke.

In Jim's profession, the sense of humor he showed was important. He always took his profession seriously. Fighting fires is not a funny business. It's one of the most dangerous jobs around and, as such, one of the most stressful.

Most of the time is spent waiting for the alarm, something firefighters hope never rings. When a firefighter does answer an alarm, it means something has gone wrong for someone, something which could turn into a tragedy in seconds. Jim saw his share of tragedies and near-tragedies during his career.

While there are things to do around the station and ways to keep busy, it's still a matter of waiting for firefighters. That waiting, having to be ready to react in an instant, creates the stress, which probably takes more of a toll than actually battling a blaze.

And that's why Jim's sense of humor, and that of the other department members, was so important. It provided a valve, a way to relieve the stress.

But apparently even Jim's broad sense of humor didn't release all the tension.

He was home Wednesday night when he collapsed. Jim was taken to the hospital, but the efforts there failed.

Jim didn't make it.

They said it appeared to be a stroke. I didn't get to talk to him Wednesday afternoon because he was busy with the other firefighters working on equipment, busy taking care of business. I wish I had visited with him now, but who could have imagined then that he wouldn't be here today. He was only 44.

But I like to think that somewhere in this vast universe that he's sitting there, sharing a laugh with those who have gone ahead. Maybe they just needed someone with a good sense of humor and a quick laugh, like Jim's.

(It was in March 1987 that Fire Chief Jim Ball passed away.)

CHAPTER 107
A RARE DIAMOND IN A ROUGH WORLD

Almost everything about Keith Hamm is big.

He's a big man blessed with a big voice, a big appetite for life, a big love for his family and friends. Now he's facing the biggest challenge of his life.

I've met Keith a few times, and I've always been impressed with him. He's always seemed happy, with himself and the world around him, even when the times themselves may not have been the happiest.

Maybe that's because of Keith's zest for life and his abiding faith. When you heard him sing -- and there are few in these parts who haven't heard Keith Hamm sing -- you got the impression he was on a first-name basis with the Good Lord. There aren't many people who can give you that impression, and not many of us have that close a relationship with the man upstairs.

Singing has been Keith's life. It's his gift, and he's never been afraid to let it shine. He loves to sing, anywhere, anytime.

There's probably not a church in the Twin Lakes Area that hasn't been blessed with his beautiful vocals. Whether an old-time gospel hymn or a contemporary Christian song, when Keith Hamm wrapped his vocal chords around it, he made it his own.

His renditions of *How Great Thou Art* and *Amazing Grace* just go straight to the center of your heart, because they're coming right out of the middle of his heart. You know he means every single one of those words when he sings them, and that he's telling you the truth.

And don't forget patriotic numbers. Stirring doesn't begin to describe the way Keith sings those. His version of *God Bless America* puts Kate Smith's to shame, and *God Bless the USA* brings tears to your eyes, a lump to your throat and makes you cheer.

He sang for *The Bulletin*'s centennial celebration in September. It was an outdoor event, and our editor, Sheila, said he told her he liked singing outside because he could really belt it out then. And that's just what he did. Nobody belts out a song like him.

Keith has a big reputation, and not just for his singing. People like being with him, probably because his happiness is contagious. He's always helped friends and been there when they needed him. He's always done whatever he could to help his community.

One story I heard was how, as a surprise for a friend, he showed up at her house during the holiday season and sang for her by the Christmas tree. What a wonderful gift.

A while back, Keith had some health problems, but he got through them with help from his friends, physical and spiritual. His illness went into remission, and the times I saw him around town, Keith seemed his usual robust self.

But the Big C is a devious foe, one that's known to sneak back on you, and that's what happened to Keith. His only enemy in the world came back, and now he's fighting it again.

As I write this, many of Keith's friends and acquaintances are preparing to sing for him. They're taking the stage and performing on his behalf as their gift to one who has so often shared his with them and the rest of the world. Keith probably would be surprised by how many friends he has, although he really shouldn't because he has touched so many people.

You're one of a kind, Keith Hamm, a rare diamond in a rough world. We're praying for you.

(Not long after this was published in 2001, Keith was called home for a command performance.)

CHAPTER 108
OLD WARRIORS

FORT HOOD, Texas – Here amidst the plains and scattered hills of central Texas, they gathered to recall old times, renew friendships and remember fallen cohorts. They came from across the country, New Jersey to Arizona and California, to this U.S. Army post, which is home to the First Cavalry Division, which was home for them.

These were the old warriors, although some weren't that old in age or spirit, and many who were certainly didn't act their age. Perhaps being among comrades and visiting with the young troopers of today's modern cavalry revitalized them.

At any rate, these were men who have given of themselves so we can continue enjoying the life, liberty and pursuit of happiness we take for granted.

It would be difficult to find a library, let alone a book, which could hold the memories of these veteran troopers. These were the men of the First Cav and all its regiments, dubbed the "First Team" by Douglas MacArthur. They were the first to go into the Admiraltys and the Philippines, where they were the first to reach Manila.

These were the troopers who fought up and down the Korean peninsula from the summer heat of the Pusan Perimeter to winter's bitter cold at Unsan. These were the men who became America's first airmobile troopers and battled in the jungles of Vietnam at Pleiku and the Ia Drang Valley.

It was an honor to be among these men, especially since one of them was my father.

This is the first time he'd ever attended a reunion of his division, and the first time he'd seen his comrades in nearly 40 years. Counting him, four members of the Eighth Cavalry Regiment's Fox Company reported for the reunion: Christopher, who works for the police department at Tucson; Coffey, retired from the post office in Oklahoma; and Houchins, a former government worker from Kentucky.

This was a chance for them to share their war stories with people who know what those who have never heard shots fired in anger will ever know. Not tales of great battles and glory, mind you, but personal anecdotes and memories of ordinary men thrust into extraordinary situations and how they faced them. Some, like Houchin's account of an encounter with a snake while getting water, were humorous. Others, such as the ones about sitting in the dark and not being able to see who's three feet away and whether they're friend or foe, weren't.

Such was the case of most of those attending the

division reunion. Friendships born serving the country, especially on the battlefield, are special ones time can't erase. There is a special camaraderie forged in those circumstances unlike most people will ever experience.

These were men who remain proud of the First Cav long after many have served with it. Whether it was a lapel pin with the division crest, or a Stetson cavalry hat festooned with crossed sabers and pins, or a fatigue jacket bearing division and unit patches, they unashamedly, and unabashedly, showed their pride in the division.

As part of the reunion activities, the old warriors got a chance to see the new troopers and their modern equipment in action. Many could be heard to say, "If we had had those, ..." as new tanks and helicopters were put through their paces. Today's military has some truly awesome firepower at its command.

But it takes more than hardware, and the spirit of the old warriors lives on in today's trooper. "Honor and Courage" remain the watchword of the Eighth Cavalry, just as "Garryowen" always shall be the call to honor for the Seventh. And to both the old and new warriors, they represent ideals that are at the heart of our way of life.

Some of the old warriors were able to acquaint themselves with some of the current generation of soldiers, and many bestowed their highest compliment upon today's troopers: They are as good, if not better, than the old warriors. Should the need arise, they'll be able to do the job.

And, since only old warriors can truly know what it's like to answer the call, they hope that need never arises for today's troopers.

(Sad to say, since this column was written, the First Cav has been through two more wars, and its troopers were able to do the job.)

CHAPTER 109
SPECIAL EVENTS
WELCOME TO THE WORLD

(On April 13, 1985, our son was born. This was a gift to him.)

S amuel Eli Garrett, you made this old world a little brighter at 5:06 p.m. Saturday.

After a long wait and some anxious hours, you finally arrived – all 8 pounds, 7 ounces and 21 ½ inches of you. Never had I seen a more beautiful sight in my life.

You had a tough time getting here, and for a little bit you had us all worried that you might not make it. But when I saw you there in the hospital nursery, your legs kicking away, your hands flailing in the air and your just opened eyes looking around to take in your new surroundings, I knew you were all right. I knew you were here to stay.

It's hard to describe all the emotions you feel on seeing your first-born for the first time. I went through more feelings in a matter of seconds than I'd ever felt before. Relief, joy, excitement, anticipation, pride, all those and more hit when I saw you.

What a sight we must have been, your grandparents and I, as we stood there at the nursery window with huge smiles and tears flooding down our faces as emotions overwhelmed us. I had never felt anything like it before.

Then, a few hours later, when your mother saw you for the first time, Eli, those emotions came rushing back. Although she was exhausted and still groggy from medication, Kim's face quickly brightened when she saw you. I'll never forget the look of love on her face as she looked at you. There are really no words to describe that look, that glow, which came over her as she realized you were all right and that everything was just perfect.

I don't know if, somewhere in your mind, you'll have memories of those early hours after your arrival, but your mother and I will always remember them. We'll always remember how beautiful you were then, knowing that, to us, at least, you'll only grow more beautiful in our eyes. We'll always remember all the folks who came by to see you, and all the people at the hospital who cared for you.

I'll also always remember those who cared for your mother during those rough hours before you were born. Without them, who knows what might have happened to you and your mother.

Each and every one of them shall always have my deepest gratitude.

While the world may seem filled with bad things to many people, for your mother and I it is filled only with happiness now. Small as you are, you've rid our world of any darkness or gloom. The light you've brought to us outshines even the sun. In the short time you've been here, you've already given us far more than we ever will be able to give you.

Now that you're here, things are just beginning for us. There is so much ahead of us, so many things to do, so many things for you to see. All the wonders of the world lie ahead of you, Eli; all its beauty and mystery, its secrets and joys, all the many and vast experiences of life. We'll be there to share many of those experiences with you, to help you learn and understand. And, undoubtedly, you'll teach us many things as well as each day goes by.

Actually, Eli, you'd be surprised at what you'll probably teach us and help us to learn and understand. You've already taught us one thing – that there is indeed a worthwhile future. It's been said a baby is God's way of telling us the world will go on. And I can't help but believe that now. As I hold you in my arms and gaze into your face, I do indeed see the future in those eyes.

Someday, you may read these words and wonder about your father. You'll probably think he's a little too sentimental, maybe a little crazy, and that he's likely to embarrass you by bursting into tears over the many achievements he's sure you'll make. Well, you're right. You mean everything to me, and if I could give you the moon and stars, I would. But all I have to offer is love, and it is a gift I readily give you.

Welcome to the world, Eli.

CHAPTER 110
WELCOME TO THE WORLD, AMELIA GARRETT

(On March 21, 1996, our daughter was born. This was a gift to her.).

It's been a while since we changed diapers in our household, but it's something we'll all be getting plenty of practice doing now that the latest little Garrett has hit the world. Amelia Morgan Garrett made her debut at 8:19 a.m. Thursday in all her 8-pound, 4-ounce glory. She announced her own arrival with a demonstration of tremendously good lungs, then proceeded to kick back, content as could be to enjoy all life has to offer her now. As far as I'm concerned, she's already got the world at her tiny feet with an entire family ready to serve her every need. That's one advantage to being a baby – no cares, no worries, no concerns as long as someone's there with a bottle and a fresh diaper.

Amelia already has big brother Eli entranced by her spell. His one wish in our having another baby was that he be the first in the family to hold her (well, he did want a Big Mac for lunch, too), and, indeed, he was the first of us to hold his new sister.

When Amelia first arrived in the nursery, you could sense Eli's uncertainty over how exactly she was going to affect life as he knows it. Feeling left out of the limelight, perhaps even a bit jealous, he'd peer through the nursery window, walk down the hall, then return for another look, his hands jammed into his jean pockets.

But all it took was that first touch, holding this brand new tiny person in his arms for Eli to put his worries to rest. Here was *his* little sister, someone for him to help care for, help protect, to love.

Oh, there undoubtedly will be the usual sibling rivalry as Eli and Amelia grow. That's only natural. But I think since he got to hold her first and played a part in her arrival, Eli may not look at Amelia quite so much as a rival but more of an ally. Now he will have someone to help him gang up on Mom and Dad.

Mom, at this point, is doing as well as can be expected. Its been a long nine months for her, and now she needs all the rest she can get, at least until Amelia goes home. Then all of us can forget rest for a while.

Seeing our child for the first time is quite an experience, you're not sure whether you ought to laugh, cry, shout with joy or jump. You just work all these together into some indecipherable emotion. That's how it was with Eli … and that's how it was with Amelia, too.

Having a daughter puts a whole new spin on

things for me. Besides having to learn how to buy toys and clothes and such for girls, I realized in only a few hours I've started thinking a bit differently as a father.

While watching Eli wolf down his promised Big Mac, I noted how some young gentlemen were commenting about various young ladies around us. In a few years – which will pass much too quickly to suit me – Amelia could be the subject of such conversation. I realized I probably wouldn't be too fond of it. As I said, a daughter puts a different spin on things, and already the protective father is coming out in me.

I just hope I'll be protective enough without being overly protective. Perhaps wrapping the house in barbed wire when she turns 16 so the boys won't come around won't be overly protective.

Seriously, however, as I look at my beautiful new daughter – and all new daughters are beautiful – I'm reminded just how wide open her future is. Just a day old, and she already has a world of opportunity before her.

I don't see any limitations for her, only horizons.

The wonderful thing about being a child, whether Eli's age or as young as Amelia, is the world can be limitless. As far as I'm concerned, both my children, and all children for that matter, can become whatever they want to be as long as they're willing to go after it.

Who knows, as rapidly as the world changes these days, Amelia and Eli may be doing something in 20 years which doesn't even exist now, not even as a glimmer in someone's imagination. Perhaps their own imaginations may be the spark for opening new frontiers.

A father's allowed to dream. It's in the Rules of Fatherhood, near the section about being overly protective of daughters.

But for now, Amelia, you're our bundle of joy, our gift of love. You have no cares to burden your tiny shoulders. Whatever the future from this day on, Amelia, you'll be the sugar and spice and everything nice that blends with Eli's snips and snails and puppy dog tails to give your Mom and me all we could ever want.

Welcome to the world, Amelia Garrett.

CHAPTER 111
FOR BETTER OR WORSE, FOR RICHER OR POORER ...

Fifty years is a long time for anything.

Especially a marriage.

That's how long my Dad and Mom have been married. Actually, 50 years and a day by the time you read this.

It really is quite an achievement to spend five decades together, especially in an era when marriage has become a revolving door for some folks. It takes a lot for two people to stick it out for 50 years, a lot of love, a lot of caring, a whole lot of patience. And a whole lot of luck.

Tommy Garrett and Frances Wilsford were married March 22, 1952, at the Miller County Courthouse in Texarkana.

Mom was born and raised in Red River County. That also was the home of author William Humphrey, who used it as a setting for his novel, *Home from the Hill*, that later became a Robert Mitchum movie that's one of our family's favorites.

Dad was born and raised in Woodruff County, down toward the White River delta country. There used to be a sign in front of a church in Augusta, the county seat, that Woodrow Wilson's family had lived here once.

Both grew up during the hard times of the Depression, although during those days in rural Arkansas and Texas it wasn't much different than the good times. Dad was the oldest child in his family, Mom was the youngest in hers. Neither made it very far in school, which wasn't unusual then, but that didn't stop Mom from being a big reader and Dad from eventually becoming a government inspector at Red River Army Depot.

Dad met Mom after he followed his uncles from Arkansas to Texas. One of his uncles, Grady, had married one of Mom's sisters, Maggie, and that led to a mixed bag of relationships for our families.

They'd met before Dad was called back into the Army and sent on a scenic tour of the lovely Korean peninsula during late 1950 and early 1951. After being severely wounded in April 1951, Dad was ultimately shipped back to an Army hospital in Texas and then discharged.

He and Mom got together again and finally decided to get hitched. Dad recalled they were married by a justice of the peace who also happened to be a minister.

Besides their getting married on March 22, another way Dad always remembered their anniversary was that their wedding came the day after a tornado ripped through Judsonia. For some reason, Dad has the uncanny habit of relating significant family events to tragedies and meteorological occurrences. (There was a thunderstorm when I was born.)

It was the start of a lifetime together, most of it lived at and around DeKalb, Texas. Dad's done many things through the years. He worked as a mechanic, which also was a hobby for him until just a few years ago. He worked on a ranch and in road construction. He finally went to work for the Department of Defense at Red River Army Depot. Dad worked in various departments there, working his way up to being an inspector.

Much of the time, Mom was what's known today as a stay-at-home-mom. Mothers could do that more readily then than now. For a while, she and Dad ran a country store. Then she went to work for King's Cleaners, where she worked for many years.

As I remember things, they always loved each other, even when things weren't rosy. I suppose that's when loving someone matters the most. There were times when they fussed with each other, getting angry at one another and not talking for a bit, although those times didn't last long. Even when they griped at one another, I always thought they respected each other, which is as important as loving one another.

They still do.

They moved to Mountain Home in the fall of

1987, planning, as they put it, to help Kim, Eli and me (and, later, Amelia). Things went well for a while, but a few years ago health problems intervened. Mom had the more serious ailments. She pretty much stays home now. Dad takes care of her, jokingly referring to his daily routine as his job. He gets out a little every day, usually for lunch and to go to the store and post office. He doesn't drive as far, or as well, as he once did.

But that's OK because Dad doesn't like getting too far away from Mom, or staying away very long.

Even after 50 years.

CHAPTER 112
HAPPY BIRTHDAY, HAPPY FATHER'S DAY, DAD

My Dad thinks that if he'd known he was going to live this long, he'd have taken better care of himself.

Well, he did the best he could considering all he's been through in the last 80 years. Dad is the first in his family to reach the age of 80, on either the Garrett or Inman side. I hope to be the second Garrett in this line to make it that far, barring unforeseen circumstances.

Of course, Dad's encountered a few of those unforeseen circumstances in his life. He was born during the Roaring '20s, although in southeast Arkansas, they didn't really notice the era. It was an area of cotton farms and floods rather than flappers and "23 skidoo."

Hard times were nothing new to the folks in that part of Arkansas when the Great Depression hit. In fact, they hardly noticed a difference.

One of Dad's earliest memories was being a child and having to stay in a railroad car on a levee because flooding forced his family from their home. In those days, flooding was common on that stretch of the White River where it goes through the Delta region.

Dad says he can recall people listening to weather reports on the radio to find out if it was raining heavily here in the Ozarks because they knew that water would be rolling their way eventually.

When it wasn't raining or flooding, Dad's family was farming, or sharecropping. That meant everyone who could worked, no matter how young they were. Dad remembers what it was like to pick cotton in the hot sun, dragging an ever-growing sack behind him between the plant rows. He also remembers what it's like to plow with a team of mules and do everything from hauling water to feeding chickens.

He says he doesn't really like chicken that much now because his family ate so much of it when he was young.

But he remembers fun times, too, such as playing baseball and getting to go to town on a Saturday. One of the big pastimes among his cousins and friends was playing pranks on one another. These days some of their pranks don't seem that funny because it seemed a lot of them wound up in good-natured fights. But I guess to a bunch of country boys, they were an amusing way to pass the time.

Dad had several jobs as a young man, including driving a truck and working on levees. He drove heavy construction equipment for a while both before and after his stint in the Army. Dad went into the service at the end of World War II, but everything was over before he got into that fight. He went into the reserves, and in 1950, got to go to a little place called Korea.

As with most veterans, Dad's wartime service was one of the biggest highpoints of his life. It still has an impact on him today. He didn't talk about it for a long time, then when he started, the stories just kept coming. Mostly they're about his comrades-in-arms in the First Cavalry and the ways they got through their time in harm's way.

Dad was lucky to come home, at least in one piece. A Chinese mortar crew dropped a shell almost on top of him. He said others in his unit only found splinters left of his rifle. He was sent back to a hospital ship, then Japan and finally to Texas to recover and rehabilitate.

It wasn't long after that that, he married Mom and they started their life together, a life that's still going 51 years later. Then a couple of years later, I came along, and no one's life has been the same since.

I have good memories of Dad, although many are of him working. That was his pastime. He raised a garden every year, a garden that kept getting bigger and bigger year after year until he was raising a small truck patch. He always worked in the garden, even when he got home at 1 in the morning after working the swing shift.

THOMAS GARRETT

He loved to work on cars, trucks, anything with
an engine. He could take them apart and put them
back together in no time, then take them part again
just to see if he could make them work better. Dad
always worked, even for recreation. He still talks
fondly of working, and how much he misses it.

These days, he talks a lot about things he
misses.

Dad's not getting around as spryly as he used to,
but he's still getting around, and that's what counts.
After all, he's seen 80 years and has earned the right
to slow down.

His birthday was Thursday, and it always falls
next to Father's Day. So, happy birthday, Dad, and
happy Father's Day. I love you.

CHAPTER 113
NEW YEAR'S LETTER TO MY GREAT-GRANDCHILDREN

To my great-grandchildren:

I'm writing this on the last day of 1999. Some say it's the last day of the 20th century, but I'm not going to get into that because it really doesn't matter in the greater scheme of the universe. Too many people with too much time on their hands have carried on about this point for way too long.

Anyway, today's paper is going into a time capsule on Mountain Home's new Arkansas State University campus and the capsule is supposed to be opened in 50 years. Personally, I plan to be there. (Look for the short dumpy guy in a hat.)

But just in case, I thought I'd send you a message.

At this writing, you haven't been born. In fact, your parents haven't even been born yet. And Grandpa Eli is just 14 while Grandma Amelia is only 3. So by the time you see this, I'll be a really old poot. (Great-grandma Kim hasn't aged a bit.)

449

THOMAS GARRETT

This is a special time as the 1900s draw to a close. At this moment there are celebrations going on all around the world as the clock strikes midnight in each time zone. People have really been looking forward to this occasion. Some are all giddy and excited about the new age dawning on us. Some have a sense of dread; they fear the end is near. Others are worried about the Y2K bug, something that by 2050 should be little more than a footnote in a history book.

Assuming you still have books.

I'm one of those who look forward to the future. I'm anxious to see what's next, what new wonders will be revealed, what technology will bring, what's just over the next hill and around the next bend. Generally I consider myself to be a pragmatic individual with a bit of optimism and a touch of cynicism thrown in to help keep things in balance. But I have to admit to being optimistic about the future.

Naturally my cynical side would say it's just because it has to be better than the past. Perhaps, although I'd prefer to think that we've learned from our past so we can avoid repeating our mistakes, which should give the future a bit of an edge. Of course, we'll undoubtedly make new mistakes, even create new ways to make them. You'll know more about that than I do. It'll be part of your history.

Seriously, I do have high hopes for the future. We humans can be more intelligent than we often

450

give ourselves credit for on the whole. Just look how far we've come technologically since the last day of 1899.

We've been flying for less than a hundred years, yet we've already sent men to the moon and back, and there are hopes of sending manned expeditions to Mars. Maybe when this time capsule is open we'll have gone to Mars, have space stations and bases on the moon. There may even be a lunar McDonald's.

When I was in college (which was a really long time ago for you) a computer could take up most of the space in a building. Now you can carry one with you that'll fit in a desk drawer and do far more than its giant predecessors ever could. With the rate of computer development now, in 50 years our computers will seem as ancient and outdated to you as an abacus.

Television is in the midst of change technologically to something called high-definition TV. It's supposed to make the images clearer and more cinematic so we can better enjoy silly sitcoms. Instead of TV, you'll probably have three-dimensional holographic images that you can interact with, like on *Star Trek*, which will probably still be in syndication.

More importantly, I anticipate there will be great strides in medical science by your time. Hopefully there will be cures for many of today's common diseases such as cancer in its many forms, AIDS, multiple sclerosis, Alzheimer's and a myriad of others. With any luck there won't have been any new ones released to plague your generation. Maybe they'll even have found a way to slow the aging process (which could account for the possibility of me still being around.)

Perhaps by your time our concerns will be more in balance with the environment. For us it's a continuing effort to protect and preserve the natural environment for you. I hope the White River is still clean and clear, with plenty of trout to catch, and that the lakes are still unspoiled and filled with loads of bass, stripers, crappie and catfish. I hope there are still plenty of woods around with lots of big trees and that there are abundant deer, squirrels, wild turkeys and other wildlife.

Most of all, I hope you have a good life. I hope you don't have to live in fear of war and violence, of drugs and crime, of petty political squabbles, of social unrest. I hope yours is a world where people can get along together, work together and care for one another, a world where people still have faith, a world better than ours.

And remember, if I'm still around when they open the time capsule look for the short, dumpy old poot in a hat.

Best wishes,
Your great-grandpa